Gardening on a Shoestring

Gardening on a Shoestring

100 ways to create a garden on a budget

Alex Mitchell

Photography by Sarah Cuttle

Kyle Books

For my grandmother, a gardening inspiration

First published in Great Britain in 2015 by
Kyle Books, an imprint of Kyle Cathie Ltd
192–198 Vauxhall Bridge Road
London SW1V 1DX
general.enquiries@kylebooks.com
www.kylebooks.com

10 9 8 7 6 5 4 3 2 1

ISBN 978 0 85783 265 8

Editor: Judith Hannam
Copy Editor: Helena Caldon
Editorial Assistant: Claire Rogers
Designer: Louise Leffler
Photographer: Sarah Cuttle
Illustrator: Rosie Scott
Production: Nic Jones, Gemma John and Lisa Pinnell

A Cataloguing in Publication record for this title is available from the British Library.

Colour reproduction by ALTA London
Printed and bound in China by Toppan Leefung Printing Ltd.

CONTENTS

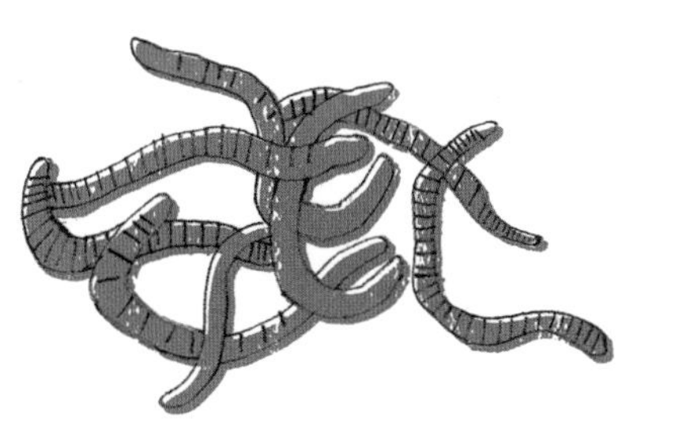

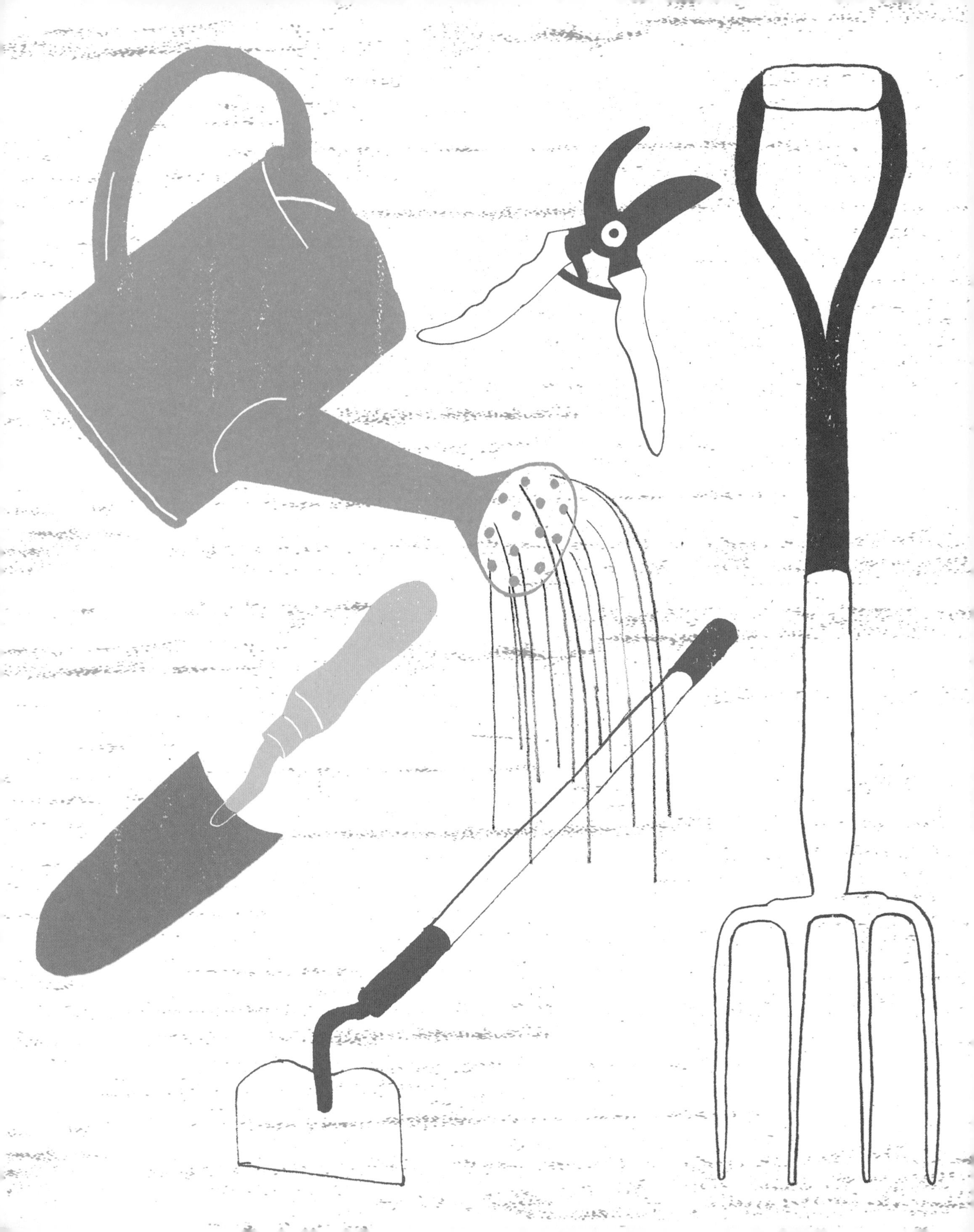

How to be a Shoestring Gardener

We've all done it – stumped up on plants, tools and endless bits of plastic kit and then thrown them at the garden in the hope that they will miraculously organise themselves into something beautiful. But you really don't need all that paraphernalia to be a successful gardener.

Sometimes you don't need to buy anything at all. From garden furniture for free to how to avoid costly florists by having your own cutting patch, there are plenty of savvy and resourceful ways to keep costs down. And even when you do put your hand in your pocket, the following tips will ensure you get the best for your cash whether it's learning how to spot healthy plants or getting a bargain at the checkout.

There's no need to be an expert. The projects in this book are all achievable, but to be sure I have given the following trowel ratings of difficulty:

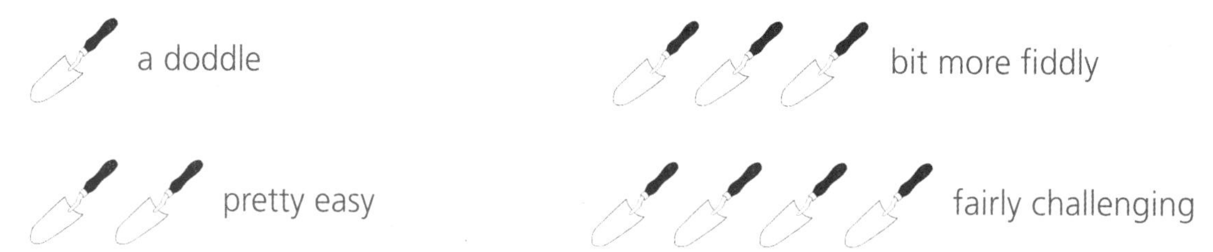

Get to know your garden

Before you even think about spending anything, make friends with your garden – sunny bits, ugly bits and all. It'll not only show you what plants you already have, but ensure that, when you do buy, you don't waste your money. After all, if you want a glamorous bougainvillea clambering up your house but live in a cool climate it will die during the first winter. If you yearn for a spread of lush hostas but have no shade they won't flourish.

Phrases such as 'right plant, right place' sound naggingly bossy, and we all try to bend the rules now and then, but to start with, play it safe with your plant choices, selecting those that prefer the conditions your garden can provide. If a plant label says 'full sun', it means it; only position these where they can get sun all day long. If a label says 'partial shade' it will be ok in an area that gets a few hours of direct sun and some dappled shade – from a tree, for example. The shade cast by a building is not partial, it's deep, so in these spots, only go for plants that say 'Partial or full shade' on their labels.

Garden knowledge: **the checklist**

- Using a compass (your smartphone probably has one), work out which way your garden faces. Stand at the back door, hold up the compass in front of you and see where the arrow is pointing. In the northern hemisphere, west- and south-facing gardens tend to be the sunniest and north- and east-facing plots less sunny (in the southern hemisphere this is reversed).

- Now look around for tall buildings or trees that could overhang your garden and cause shady areas within it. Remember that the sun rises roughly in the east and sets in the west; think about how this might create shifting areas of sun and shade throughout your garden over the course of the day. Remember, too, that the sun is higher in the sky in the summer so some areas may be more shady in the winter than in summer.

- Next think about wind. Is your garden sheltered? Is there a fence or wall that protects it from wind, or do shrubs in your garden tend to blow around when it gets blustery? Is the area closer to the house more sheltered than the bottom of the garden, for example?

- Where is your garden, geographically? Do you get many frosts over winter? Coastal areas often avoid frosts but instead tend to be windy. Urban gardens can be several degrees warmer than those in the countryside.

- Is your garden flat or slopey? The area at the bottom of a slope can be a lot colder than that at the top because cold air travels downhill – especially if there is nowhere for it to escape to (which is why old, sloped, walled gardens always had a door in the lower wall).

- Now get to know your soil. Pick up a handful of earth and squeeze it. If it feels gritty and crumbles easily when you try to shape it into a ball, it most likely has a high sand content. If it can be made into a ball or even a rope, it has a higher clay content. If it has a whiteish look to it, it is probably chalky. Sandy soils are termed light soils, clay soils are known as heavy soils. Bear this in mind when choosing plants because they all prefer different types of soil. A good plant label should tell you what sort of soil a plant likes.

- Look at the plants that are already in your garden and are thriving. Take your cue from these and also your neighbours' gardens and what is growing in the local area. If their plants are established and happy, you know the conditions are right for them here. Some soils are naturally acidic, some more alkaline; if you see blue hydrangeas everywhere, for example, you know you have a naturally acidic soil.

Prune before you pulverise

Many of us move into houses that have established, overgrown gardens. We see tangly climbers and gargantuan bushes blocking views and shading areas and we immediately panic and pull out everything. Typically we are then left with a bald, featureless garden. Too late we might realise that that large evergreen bush was actually doing a rather useful job hiding next door's wheelie bins. Too late we realise that a bare wooden fence looks a bit, well, bare. So then off we go to the garden centre and load our trolley with more climbers and shrubs to fill the gaps we have left, and we replace the established climbers and shrubs with smaller specimens – often of the very same plant we ripped out – which will take years to look good. Doesn't make much sense, does it?

Most overgrown bushes and climbers can be rehabilitated with a bit of pruning, which will get them back in shape. With a bit of care you can turn that saggy old bay tree into an elegant sphere, or lop off the lower branches of large shrubs or trees to let in more light. So get out your secateurs rather than your wheelbarrow – there may be life in the old dog(rose) yet...

Move it, don't lose it

Sometimes the problem is not the plant but where it is. Rather than hoiking out and throwing away a plant that is in the way, consider if you could move it somewhere else in the garden where it would be better suited. It is least disturbing for an established plant if you move it in late winter or early spring; doing so then will give it the best chance of survival. Always give the plant a good mulch of garden compost once you have replanted it.

Plants you can cut down to within 30cm of ground level

- *Abelia x grandiflora*
- Clematis
- Cotoneaster
- Ivy
- Osmanthus
- Wisteria
- Rose
- Pyracanthus

Plants you can cut down to within 60cm of ground level

- Jasmine
- Honeysuckle
- Russian vine

Plants to cut back to within a framework of branches

Prune these stems back to a bud or a main branch.

- Passionflower
- Escallonia
- Callistemon

Plants to cut back gradually over a few years

Each year, cut one in three stems to ground level, reducing the others by half.

- Forsythia
- Hydrangea
- Magnolia

Weed it and reap

Many beginner gardeners are worried they don't know the difference between a weed and a plant that is supposed to be there, so they either leave everything or pull it all out. Underneath all those nettles, annual dog mercury and ground elder there could be lurking some hidden treasures – beautiful plants just hoping to be revealed. Do a search online for common garden weeds in your part of the country and you will have plenty of photographs to refer to. Then you can weed away in confidence, leaving anything else there to flourish. If in further doubt, ask a more knowledgeable neighbour or relative.

It's not only plants you may uncover under the weeds and overgrown grass. If a garden has had several owners there could be all manner of exciting and useful treasures waiting to be found that could be reused, such as paving slabs, bricks and pots.

Savvy Tip

Websites that contain images of seedlings are particularly useful when weeding – theseedsite.co.uk has 800 photographs of the first stages of various garden plants so you can identify whether that plant you just uncovered is weed or wonder.

Make ugly features disappear

A coat of paint can be a miraculous thing. If you have an unsightly garden building, fence or wall you can make it blend into the background if you paint it dark grey. Hey presto, it will all but disappear. Much cheaper than replacing it.

Beg before you buy

It's easy to obtain many beautiful garden plants for free if you take cuttings, collect seeds or divide mature plants. Sometimes this can give you pretty much an instant flowerbed. Next time you visit relatives, friends or neighbours, take a quick look around their garden and see if there are any plants you can pilfer. See How to Make New Plants for Free for more tips, page 108.

When you buy...

It's easy to get carried away when buying plants, but follow these easy pointers and you can let your imagination run wild without spending more than you have to.

Seedy savings

Many plants grow very easily and quickly from seed. A packet containing about 100 seeds can cost you a fifth of the price of one plant. It's not difficult to do the maths on this one. Annuals – flowering plants that germinate, flower and die in one year – are prime candidates for growing from seed and you can easily fill a bare border with a riot of colour in just a couple of months. See the box opposite for some common annuals that you can easily grow from seed. From mid-spring to early summer, simply scatter them directly onto finely-raked garden soil in a sunny spot, rake them in and water well. Once they have set seed you could even save it to sow next year (see page 110).

Easy annuals to grow from seed

Nasturtiums
Sweet peas
Cosmos
Love-in-a-mist (*Nigella damascena*)
Flowering tobacco (*Nicotiana sylvestris*)
Marigold (*Calendula*)
Cornflowers (*Centaurea cyanus*)
Californian poppy (*Eschscholzia californica*)
Bishop's flower (*Ammi majus*)

How not to waste money online...

Buying plants online is great fun and so easy; no trudging around pushing a trolley down endless alphabetised aisles, no frustration when you can't find something – just click and wait for the knock at the door. But here are a few tips to make sure you don't spend more than you have to...

Select a safe spot. When ordering, make sure you give an alternative location where the package can be left if you are not at home when it is delivered. Plants won't last long sitting packaged up in a hot sorting office, and the last thing you want is a cardboard box of dead plants you will have to re-order at more expense.

Club together. Online purchases come with courier or postage costs, so it pays to group your purchases so you only have to pay this once. If you have friends who might want plants too, think about sharing a delivery – sometimes there are bargains to be had if you order a multiple of one specific plant.

Shop around. The larger online companies are often good value, but don't rule out small specialist nurseries – especially if you are buying roses, fruit trees or hedging plants – and sellers on eBay.

How big? Don't forget to check the size of the pot before you order. Plants sold online are usually shown by pot size – from a 9cm pot for small plants, such as herbs, all the way up to 12 litres for a tree. Remember to compare like with like when shopping around – that shrub may not be such a bargain when you realise it's the size of a matchbox!

Think ahead. Don't forget that plants can grow pretty quickly. Smaller specimens may not only be cheaper than large ones but also might establish more easily and therefore will soon catch up. A larger root ball is more vulnerable to drying out than a small one.

Build up slowly. It easy to build up a collection of plants by taking cuttings or dividing them (see How to make Plants for Free, p108). If you are prepared to wait a few years for your garden to mature, save your money now and buy only a few plants of each variety. Then make new plants from them when they are established. Stem cuttings can be taken almost straight away so you may not have to wait as long as you think.

Wait and see. Suppliers often put together offers, especially at the end of the season. This is particularly the case with bare-root plants such as fruit trees and hedging that have to be planted in the dormant season. Keep your eye on the price on suppliers' websites and you'll see the price fall week by week as spring nears. Time it right and you can make major savings and still get your hedging or fruit trees in time.

right Californian poppies are easy to grow from seed.

... and in garden centres and nurseries

Most of us head to dedicated garden centres or nurseries when we want to fill our car boot with plants. But don't rule out cut-price pound stores that often have a surprisingly good and affordable range of seeds and fruit bushes. Car boot fairs and yard sales are also worth keeping an eye out for.

Savvy Tip

When shopping, don't be too distracted by gorgeous flowers. Garden centres put out displays of the plants that are looking good at the moment and it's tempting to buy them. But remember, if they're in full flower now they might have finished flowering in a week or even days. Look for plants with unopened flower buds rather than the ones in full flower. Even better, when buying shrubs and perennials, try to wait until the end of summer into winter when garden centres discount their stock. Autumn is a good time for planting and they'll be up and running the following spring having already settled into their new home.

Buy healthy plants: **the checklist**

- Trust your instincts: If a plant doesn't look healthy, don't buy it. Trying to nurture a sickly looking specimen back to health isn't worth the hassle and it could even bring in disease to your other plants. Avoid any plants with brown or curling leaves, dead bits or dark-spotted foliage. Sticky leaves (a sign of aphids) or webbing (spider mite) are also things to be wary of.

- Turn the pot over and look for roots coming out of the bottom. If they have formed a mat that would make it difficult to remove the plant from the pot, it is pot-bound and you're better off choosing another.

- Take the plant out of its pot and look at the roots. If they have circled around the inside of the pot making a dense spiral, choose another. The plant is pot-bound and these roots won't find it easy to spread out and grow once it is planted out into the soil.

- Moss, weeds, liverwort and lichen growing on the surface of the compost in a potted plant are signs that a plant has been in its container for too long. It's not necessarily a deal breaker, but if you do buy a plant like this, scrape off the top couple of centimetres of compost before planting it out to avoid spreading moulds and weed seeds.

Planting out

Here's how to give a plant the best start in life.

Dig a hole with a trowel or garden spade slightly larger than the root ball of the plant.

Turn the plant upside down and, with one hand gently supporting it from the bottom, lift off the pot. Be careful not to damage the plant with the fingers of your bottom hand, avoiding touching the stems or buds if at all possible. A splayed hand, gently supporting the compost from below, is the way to go. If the plant won't come out of the pot, squeeze the pot slightly or, if the pot isn't flexible, try poking a stick through the drainage holes to push it out.

Before you plant it, check there are no weed seedlings growing around the base of the plant, removing any you do see. If there is a layer of liverwort (see left), remove this with your fingers.

Tease out the root ball a little with your fingers so that the roots can spread out easily in their new home. If they are very congested and have spiralled around the inside pot, try to 'unwind' as many as you can without damaging them.

Set the plant into the hole you have made, making sure it is exactly the same level it was in the pot. Too deep and it may become waterlogged, too high and the roots may dry out. If you are unsure, lay a stick across the planting hole to determine the level.

Once you are happy with the level, backfill the hole with the soil you took out, making sure it doesn't contain any large stones or clods. Push down firmly either with your hands or feet, depending on the size of the plant, taking care not to damage the plant itself. Water well and leave to get on with it.

Fill your house with flowers without spending a fortune

A cutting garden – a patch of flowers grown exclusively for cutting and filling vases in the house – sounds like a luxury, but any reasonably sized garden has room for one. All you need is a 2 x 3m patch of soil . If you're a fan of cut flowers, creating a flower garden will save you a fortune on buying them. Your windowsills will be resplendent with blooms all summer, your friends will be thrilled with your flowering gifts and you won't have to rob the rest of your garden to do it.

This mix of seeds ensures a beautiful supply of flowers and foliage from midsummer right through to the first frosts. It's just a suggestion, though; look online for cutting-garden seed collections and particularly those aimed at smaller gardens – they are often very good value.

You will need

An area of ground 2 x 3m, cleared of weeds and stones and raked to a fine tilth
Tape measure
Garden twine
Twigs or sticks
Scissors
6 packets of seed: *Bupleurum griffithii, Rudbeckia hirta* 'Marmalade', *Cosmos* 'Sensation Mixed', Cornflower 'Blue Ball', *Ammi majus, Agrostemma githago* (Corncockle).
Rake
Watering can with rose attachment/garden hose

When to do it

Mid- to late spring

How to do it

Divide your growing area into six equal squares, staking out the grid with twine tied to sticks pushed into the soil. Then sow each square with a different variety of seed. Rake over the soil gently to cover the seeds and water well. Keep the patch weeded and protect the young shoots from slugs and snails until established.

left Sowing each variety of seed in a different square makes harvesting and weeding easier.
right Cut flowers throughout the summer to keep the plants blooming.

How not to spend a fortune on garden furniture

Furniture for the garden can be very expensive, especially if it is built to last and designed to be left outside all year round. You will pay a premium for sustainable hardwood furniture and for many it is well worth the investment since it will last for years and you won't have to lug it in and out of storage. Buying more affordable softwood furniture that needs to be kept under cover during inclement weather can be a false investment because you'll often find you have to repaint or even replace it after a couple of years. Plastic furniture or even indoor tables and chairs brought outside temporarily are a reasonable alternative if budget is an issue. But you can also make surprisingly attractive, long-lasting garden furniture yourself for just the cost of some paint. Here are a couple of ideas...

Make a garden table out of pallets

Wooden pallets are used for lifting and transporting anything from food to bricks. Many stores have a stack of pallets out the back and most will, if asked, be happy to let you have a few for nothing. Pallets are a great source of free timber and, with a bit of sanding and a few coats of paint, can be upcycled into some surprisingly smart furniture. This low coffee table is perfect for a patio, deck, roof garden or balcony.

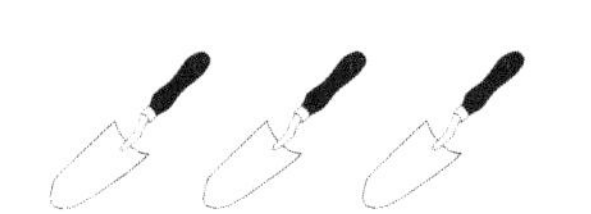

You will need
Claw hammer
2 identical wooden pallets
Sandpaper
Exterior wood paint
Paintbrush
Exterior wood glue
4 bricks as weights

When to do it
Any time of year in dry weather

How to do it
Using your claw hammer, take apart one of the pallets to extract the wooden blocks that hold the two layers together. Put them to one side. Now sand down the other pallet so it is smooth and give it and the blocks two coats of exterior wood paint.

Once dry, turn the pallet over and glue a wooden block to each corner to make the legs. Weigh the blocks down with bricks to make them secure. Once dry, repeat with four more blocks. Once completely dry, turn the table upright.

How to make garden stools from car tyres

These hardwearing stools have a sense of humour and a modern aesthetic – and will also double as storage boxes for garden equipment. You can easily get hold of old car tyres if you ask at a tyre depot; choose the thickest ones you can find, since they need to be comfortable to sit on. Either leave the tyres unpainted for a pared-down industrial look or spray paint them for a cleaner vibe. Go for a base coat of line spray paint – the stuff they use to paint lines on the road – with a specialist rubber spray paint on top to seal it and stop it flaking off.

You will need

A car tyre
Groundsheet or other protective sheet
Line spray paint and rubber spray paint, such as Plasti Dip (optional)
1 round wooden decking tile the same circumference as the inner rim of the tyre (if you can't find a round one, use a square one and round off the corners with a hacksaw)
Exterior wood paint (optional)

When to do it

All year round in dry weather

How to do it

If painting the tyre, lay it on a groundsheet or other protective sheet and spray the outside with the line spray. Don't worry about painting the base since this will be on the ground so you won't see it. Once dry, spray another couple of coats with the rubber spray paint. Next, paint the decking tile with the wood paint. Once dry, simply place the tile inside the tyre so it is secure.

PLES

Pots for a Pittance

Container gardens can be anything you want them to be. The one thing they don't have to be is expensive. Rules are few; imagination is everything. You can make a jungle in a courtyard, a cottage garden on a balcony or a desert landscape on a roof. Express yourself, upcycle, recycle, make from scratch or just buy plants and pots for peanuts.

Upcycling on the up

Upcycling old containers such as tins and bowls to use as planters gives your garden instant character and individuality. There are plenty of vintage enamel bowls and tin baths for sale out there in upmarket garden and homeware shops, but buy those and you'll inevitably pay over the odds. Boot fairs are a good alternative source for these containers – and much more affordable – and even antique fairs can be surprisingly good value compared to retailers. These fairs are where many small traders buy their wares in the first place, so you'll be saving yourself the mark-up. They're also great fun to visit. Look online for one that is on near you.

If vintage isn't your style, there's a whole host of other options in thrift stores, where the plastic storage crate is king. Anything that looks like a pot can be a pot, as long as you add drainage holes to the base. If brightly coloured plastic doesn't offend your senses, you can grow a very successful garden in these large and very cheap receptacles – from tub trugs with handles to bins, paddling pools and laundry baskets. Or simply put plastic containers inside hessian coffee or potato sacks for a more natural look.

Sometimes upcycled containers don't even need to be purchased at all. The cupboard under the stairs or the garden shed can be full of potential treasures for the garden upcycler. If you live in a city or town, look out for restaurants throwing out large tomato and pepper tins. Delis get through huge tins of olive oil and these can be colourful and hardwearing. Vintage tins are particularly attractive, but even modern tin cans can have an industrial flair if you take off the labels and let them rust naturally. Greengrocers are a great source of containers since they have a constant supply of plywood boxes and shallow plastic mesh trays – both ideal for growing vegetables and salads in.

The best, most rewarding upcycled pot is one you make from something you're about to throw away. Whether it's a juice carton, dented colander or broken wicker wastepaper basket, there will usually be a use for it somewhere in the garden. There is something particularly satisfying about seeing geraniums thrive where you used to throw scrunched-up paper.

From metal bread tins to colanders, pretty much any container can be used to grow plants – so let your imagination run free.

The happy pot: ten tips for keeping plants healthy in containers

1. The bigger the pot, the less you will need to water it.

2. Check you have enough drainage holes in the bottom of your pot and that they are not blocked by roots or stones.

3. Add grit to the compost to allow water to drain through and prevent soggy roots.

4. Mulch the surface of the compost with shingle or gravel; it retains water and keeps roots cool in summer and prevents them rotting in winter.

5. Really drench plants – a sprinkle with the hose will just encourage roots to be shallow and more prone to drying out.

6. For very shallow containers, such as hanging baskets or shallow trays, add a handful of water-retaining gel granules or line the bottom with an old woollen jumper.

7. Watch out for weeds – every year remove the top inch of compost and replace it with fresh compost to cut down on pernicious weeds like creeping oxalis.

8. When you plant out purchases from nurseries, look for weeds and lichen on the compost surface, then remove the top layer of soil to avoid bringing weeds and moulds into your garden.

9. Don't be tempted to skimp on potting compost. This stuff is the only thing keeping your plants alive, so the better it is the happier your plants will be. Tempting as it might be to save money by buying cheap compost, chances are it will be low on nutrients. So go for a good-quality, organic, multipurpose, peat-free compost for short-term plants and a soil-based compost (such as John Innes No 2 or 3) for long-term plants, trees and perennial herbs.

10. Don't forget to feed your plants; plants will exhaust nutrients in compost after about 6 weeks, so after that the only feed they get will be from you. (See How to Make Your Own Plant Feeds, p145.)

How to water pots

Lovely as potted plants are, they take a lot of watering. You can spend up to 40 minutes a day just keeping the containers on an average terrace watered in summer, and we don't all have time for that. Risk underwatering them, however, and you'll end up with dead plants. And dead plants need replacing, which costs money.

Sometimes when you water pots with a hose or watering can you find that the water runs off the surface before it has soaked in, meaning you have to stand there repeating the exercise ad nauseam. It's always worth leaving a few centimetres of space between the top of the compost and the rim of the pot to avoid this problem.

There are plenty of irrigation kits available to buy, but many are overly complicated, including fiddly nozzles and digital timers that make them unnecessarily expensive. So save yourself from being a slave to the watering can with these affordable DIY watering systems.

The water-bottle watering system

Large pots containing trees, shrubs or perennials need a lot of water, particularly in hot weather. Even a large pot can dry out completely in under a week if not watered generously, and rainfall makes little difference since the leaf canopies of established plants often prevent the vital water reaching the compost.

Luckily, plastic 1-litre bottles can come in handy here. Simply unscrew and discard the lid, then cut off the base of the bottle and push it, lid end down, into the compost beside your plant. When the bottle doesn't fall over, it's deep enough. Fill the bottle with water and it will drip out gradually, delivering water where it is needed, direct to the plant roots. You'll waste less water through evaporation and spillages and save yourself a lot of time too.

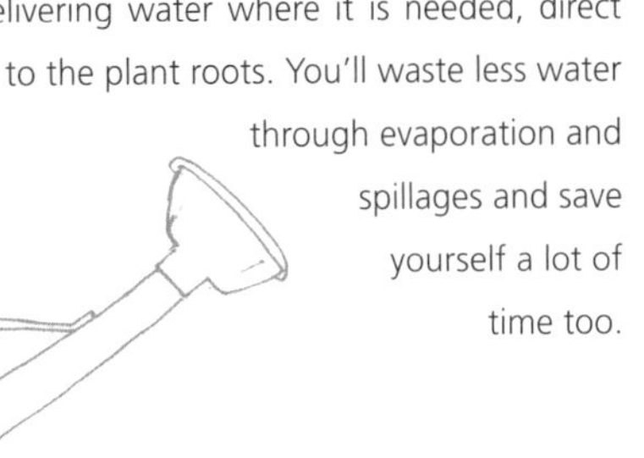

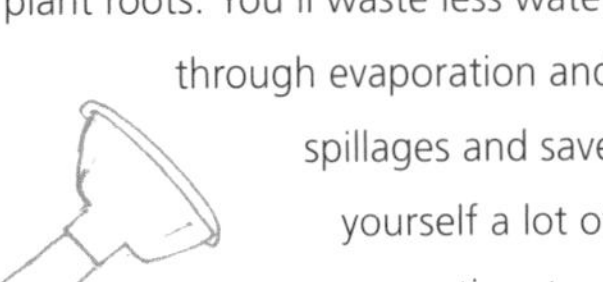

The invisible watering system

This watering system is ideal for any large pot or container, and is particularly good for moisture-loving flowering plants, fruit trees and bushes and vegetables, since it results in permanently damp compost. It's great for fig trees, raspberries, tomatoes and any plant that benefits from a regular, even supply of water. Since the water comes from underneath, little moisture is lost through evaporation – even on hot days.

This simple irrigation method is perfect for keeping plants happy when you are on holiday or on a weekend away. All you have to do is top up the reservoir every week or so until the water starts coming back up the tube, signalling that it is full. (You can add liquid plant feed to the reservoir too, if necessary.)

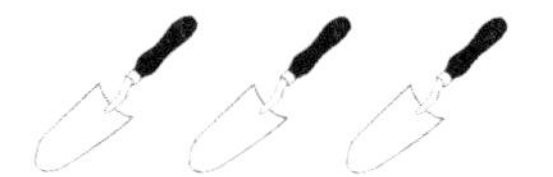

You will need

1 relatively flat, robust, plastic container with a lid that will fit in the base of your pot – a Tupperware or ice-cream tub is ideal. It must be strong enough to withstand the weight of the compost

1 large pot to grow your plant in

1 small plastic plant pot – around 9cm diameter

A sharp Stanley or craft knife

1 pair of old tights

Scissors

1 elastic band

Multipurpose or soil-based compost

1 section of plastic piping such as garden hose or irrigation pipe around 30cm in length (a larger circumference pipe is easier to fill than a narrow one – it can be flexible or rigid)

How to do it

Check your container (Tupperware or similar) fits snugly in the base of your large pot. This will act as your reservoir. Take your small plastic plant pot and cut small holes – around 6 to 8 – out of the sides using your knife. This will act as your wick. Place the pot on the lid of your container, draw around it and cut out the circle with the knife. Push the plant pot into the hole so it is a tight, snug fit, adjusting the size of the hole as necessary.

Then cut the foot off your tights with scissors and line the inside of the small plastic pot with it, securing it around the edge with an elastic band. This material acts as a filter to stop compost getting into the reservoir and silting it up. Next, fill the small wick pot with compost, pressing it down hard so it fills it completely with no air holes. Push the pot down into the reservoir so the bottom of the wick pot is a few centimetres above the base of the reservoir pot.

Next take your section of pipe, place one end vertically onto the reservoir lid and draw around it. Cut out this circle then push in the pipe so it fits snugly. This will act as your water pipe to keep the reservoir topped up. Place the whole thing in the bottom of a large pot. Fill the reservoir with water through your water pipe so it is full up. After a few minutes the surface of the compost in the wick pot should be moist. Then fill the large pot with compost and plant as normal, making sure the end of the watering pipe is poking up and not covered so you can fill it. Trim it if it is too long. If you don't like the look of the pipe, it's easy to disguise it with some planting.

You know when you have filled the reservoir when water starts coming back up the pipe. Keep it topped up every week.

1. Cut holes in the sides of the pot.
2. Place the pot on the lid of your flat container and draw around it.
3. Cut out a circle, push in the pot and line the inside with the tights, securing with a rubber band.
4. Fill the small pot with compost.
5. Cut a hole for the pipe and push it in.
6. Place the whole system at the bottom of a large pot and cover with compost.
7. Fill container through the water pipe.
8. Plant as normal.

Give a cheap terracotta pot some class

With the day-glo orange tone of a reality TV star's spray tan, mass-produced terracotta pots can look like they've come straight from the factory, but their modest price tag makes them extremely appealing to the savvy gardener. They are cheaper because they're moulded as opposed to hand-thrown and the clay used tends to be more orange in colour than that used in the handmade, more expensive versions.

In time all terracotta will weather, but if you want to speed up the process it's very easy to tone down the orange of the more affordable new pots and make them look like they've been in your garden for decades. All you really need is a couple of materials you might already have at home.

A brush with baking powder can make a new orange pot look like it's been on a sunny terrace for decades.

How to age a terracotta pot

Some people paint yogurt onto their pots to encourage moulds to grow there, giving the clay a greenish tone, but if you do this what you'll also get is patches of furry mould. An arguably more aesthetically pleasing technique lightens the clay so that it mimics a handmade finish and the natural leaching of minerals that gives pots a whiteish patina. All you need is some baking powder and spray varnish and you can create something that looks as though it's been on a sunny terrace for a decade.

You will need

Baking powder
Mixing bowl
Paintbrush
1 cheap terracotta pot
A dry stiff brush, such as a washing-up brush
1 can of hairspray, fixative or clear matt varnish suitable for exterior use

How to do it

Mix the baking powder together with some water in the bowl at a ratio of about 2 to 1 so it makes a paste. Paint this onto your pot thickly, including on the inside rim. Leave to dry completely. Using the dry stiff brush, brush off the excess powder to leave a whiteish patina. Then spray the pot all over the outside and inside with the hairspray, fixative or varnish to prevent rain washing off the powder.

right
1. Mix baking powder with water to make a paste.
2. Brush the paste onto the pot.
3. Paint the whole of the outside as well as the inside rim.
4. Leave to dry then brush off the excess powder.
5. Spray with fixative, varnish or hairspray.

1
2
3
4
5

Pots with panache:
Three container-garden style tricks

1. Less is more – select a theme for your design and your container garden will look all the better for it. Mixing metal, plastic, terracotta and wood, especially if you're using upcycled containers, could make your garden look more fly-tipped than fantastic. If you're going for bright, garish plastic containers, keep the colours harmonious with each other and bear in mind they will stand out rather than blend in. When choosing materials think about your site; modern shiny metal or bright colours may suit a city apartment balcony, but dented metal and wood are more at home in a rural, gravelled courtyard garden.

2. Make the most of your space by placing your pots on different levels. Rather than buying expensive staging or shelving, look out for cheap old stepladders in junkyards or car boot fairs. The more battered and worn they are, the more character they'll have and your herbs and other plants will look wonderful on their step stage.

3. Get creative with window boxes and hanging baskets. Choose wicker baskets for a more traditional look, or use a colander or a container made from man-made materials for a modern, unique style. In smaller spaces, such as balconies, hang planted-up bottles and tins from railings or vertical spaces. Window boxes don't have to be plastic and boring either, use any narrow container that fits the space or look out for unusual old items like bread tins, trays or wooden troughs.

above left A second-hand step ladder makes an ideal stage for pots of herbs, chillis and flowers.
above right Make the most of vertical space by attaching containers to railings, fences and walls.

Polystyrene style

Polystyrene boxes are ideal as planters in all sorts of spaces, and because polystyrene is light it insulates the soil and creates warm conditions that plants love. Deep boxes are ideal for moisture-loving plants while long, narrow trays are perfect as window boxes. As long as you don't chip or damage them, polystyrene planters will last a couple of years at least and can be left outside in all weathers. Greengrocers and fishmongers use polystyrene boxes all the time to transport their goods, and will probably be happy to have them taken off their hands if you ask nicely. Also keep an eye out for polystyrene packaging and boxes when you buy goods online.

Garish white polystyrene is not everyone's idea of a style statement though, especially when, over time, green algae forms on the surface. Luckily it's easy to paint polystyrene to smarten it up. Bright colours will give the box a vibrant, modern look while paler tones such as olive will make it blend in with natural materials.

You will need

1 polystyrene box
Latex or acrylic primer
1 paintbrush
Masonry paint or radiator paint (do not use spray paints since these can dissolve the polystyrene)
1 sharp Stanley or craft knife
Multipurpose peat-free organic compost (avoid soil-based composts since they may be too heavy)
Plant of choice

When to do it

Any time of year

How to do it

Paint the outside and inner rim of the box with the primer, making sure to cover as much of the inner edge as might be visible when planted. You may need to apply two coats to cover the markings of the polystyrene. Leave to dry, then apply your top coat of masonry or radiator paint. Cut drainage holes in the bottom of the polystyrene with your knife. Fill the pot with compost and plant as usual.

right Polystyrene is light, insulates the soil and creates warm conditions that plants love. Deep boxes are ideal for moisture-loving plants while long, narrow trays are perfect as window boxes.

Lavender in a bucket

Everyone loves lavender and it's a perfect container plant, living happily in confined conditions for several years before it becomes woody and needs to be replaced. Once your plant is about four years old, you may want to take cuttings from it for 'the next generation' (see Taking Stem Cuttings, page 116).

The key to successfully growing lavender is providing it with a sunny position and good drainage – they hate shade and soggy roots. So make sure your pot has decent drainage holes and is filled with a soil-based compost mixed with about one-third horticultural grit.

Old metal buckets are a steal if you pick them up from junk stores or antique markets. You can get lovely old dented ones for the price of a sandwich and the handle makes them so easy to carry plants around. If buckets are bashed and have holes in the bottom, so much the better, as it will save you making drainage holes. An old bucket is the perfect size for a lavender plant, but choose a compact variety of lavender, since it won't get too sprawly. French lavender, with its distinctive butterfly wing petals emerging from the top, looks particularly good, or you can't go wrong with the intense cerise-blue of 'Hidcote'.

You will need

Hammer and a large nail (optional)
1 old bucket
Horticultural grit
Soil-based compost such as John Innes No.2
1 container to mix your compost in
1 lavender plant

When to do it

Spring to autumn

How to do it

With your hammer and nail, pierce at least five holes in the bottom of the bucket, if necessary. Wiggle the nail around a bit to make sure they are as big as possible to prevent water collecting at the bottom. Add a couple of handfuls of grit to the bottom of the bucket. Pour compost and grit into a separate container at a proportion of 3 parts compost to 1 part grit and mix together with your hands. Add this to your bucket until it's two-thirds full, then position your lavender plant. Fill in around the plant with more compost and top dress with grit. Water well and put the pot in the sunniest spot you can find.

How to prevent containers falling apart

Months or years of damp compost can take their toll on an upcycled container. Wood will rot and ungalvanised metal will rust and become brittle. To some extent this is inevitable – these objects were not designed for being planted up with pansies, after all. Sometimes it adds to the charm, but if your wooden or rustable metal container is in danger of falling apart, line the inside with plastic – old compost bags or bin bags are ideal – which will keep the sides relatively dry. When you make drainage holes in the plastic liner at the base, try siting them as much as possible over any holes or gaps in the outer container; this keeps the base material as dry as possible. Raising containers off the ground on bricks or stones will prevent them sitting in damp conditions and rotting.

Metal dustbins make great containers for trees; they are big enough to hold a decent amount of compost but lightweight enough to move around. Get three and line them up to make quite a statement. You can pick up bins for a reasonable price from home stores or thrift shops. Just be sure to secure them so they don't topple over, though – putting a few bricks in the base once you've decided on their location should keep them grounded.

A pelargonium tin wall

Whether you go for traditional red, pale pink or deep magenta, the seemingly endless flowers and subtly scented leaves of pelargoniums create a happy mood. Urban courtyard gardens, roof gardens and balconies in particular are perfect locations for this potted escapism. Pelargoniums are not entirely hardy in cooler climates so people usually buy them in spring every year or keep them going in a greenhouse or kitchen windowsill over winter.

This project is a quirky, modern take on the classic terracotta wall planters you see in Mediterranean villages. Dotting a vertical surface with shiny metal cans planted with brightly coloured pelargoniums looks surprisingly effective and the containers are completely free. Leaving the cans unpainted gives a nice, minimalist, industrial look. They will rust over time, so if you want them to be shiny, coat them with some exterior rust-proof metal paint or with masonry paint for a softer aesthetic. The bigger the can, the less frequently you will have to water the plants. It's worth asking at pizza restaurants or delis to see if they have any large catering-sized cans out the back, but if not, use ordinary tins from the supermarket and plant them up with drought-tolerant plants such as pelargoniums, sempervivums, sedums or cacti.

You will need

Kitchen roll
White spirit
10 clean, empty tin cans with the labels soaked off, preferably all the same size
1 power drill with 5mm metal drill bit (if mounting on a wall)
10 rawl plugs and 10 galvanised screws (if mounting on a wall)
Screwdriver (if mounting on a wall)
10 nails (if mounting on a wooden fence)
Hammer and nail to make holes in the cans
Masonry paint/metal paint (optional)
Paintbrush (optional)
Soil-based compost such as John Innes No. 2 mixed 2 parts to 1 with horticultural grit
10 pelargonium plants

When to do it

Spring–summer

How to do it

Using kitchen roll and white spirit, rub away any remaining glue left by the labels on the cans then rinse well under running water. Next, decide on the best location for your tin wall – behind a table as a focal point is good, or perhaps on the fence down a side return (the passageway down the side of a house) that could do with brightening up. Then mark on the fence or wall with a pencil where you want each can to go. A diagonal pattern, such as that of five spots on a dice, looks effective. Drill a hole in the wall in each spot, tap in a rawl plug and screw in a galvanised screw, leaving it a centimetre proud. If you are attaching the cans to a wooden fence, simply tap in a nail.

Turn the cans upside down and pierce holes in the base of each with your hammer and nail – about 3 per can should do. Then make a further hole towards the top of the can. This hole needs to be slightly larger than the head of the screws or nails that you are hanging them up with so you might need to wiggle the nail around a bit. Paint the outside of the cans if you are doing this. Now fill your can with compost and plant each one with a pelargonium. Water well.

To mount the cans on the wall, simply hang them onto the screws or nails, checking they are secure.

Pelargoniums are fairly drought resistant but since tin cans are small, the compost will soon dry out. Water them every couple of days in hot weather and deadhead the plants as necessary to encourage them to produce new flowers.

Cosmos in a crate

The daisy-like flowers of cosmos are uncomplicated, colourful and unmistakably cheerful. Better still, they will flower for weeks on end right up to the first frosts if you keep deadheading them. You can buy cosmos plants from every garden centre under the sun, but if you grow them from seed you not only save money but also end up with more natural, elegant-looking plants rather than the slightly offputting muscular nursery-raised specimens. Choose a packet of mixed-colour seeds and you will end up with a lovely jumble of pinks and purples that will bring a hint of the meadow to any garden – even a city balcony.

Wooden crates and boxes always look good in a garden setting and the lettering on the side is all part of the charm. The cheerful chaos of cosmos in particular makes a nice contrast with the geometric shape of the crate. Of course, remind yourself that these are temporary containers – two or three years at most – so you won't be disappointed when the bottom rots and falls off (see How to Prevent Containers Falling Apart, page 33). Old fruit crates are particularly rigid and long-lasting if you can get hold of a cheap supply of them, but be aware, shops are wising up to their retro appeal so don't expect bargains everywhere. Another option is wine crates, if you can find a friendly wine merchant willing to part with them for free.

You will need

1 wooden crate
A couple of bricks or blocks to stand the crate on
1 piece of plastic pond liner, bin bag or an old compost bag
Scissors
Multipurpose organic peat-free compost
1 packet of cosmos seeds – try 'Sensation Mixed' for tall mixed colours

When to do it

Mid-spring to early summer

How to do it

Once planted up, your crate will be heavy, so it is best to get it into position first. Place it in a sunny spot, propping it up on a couple of bricks. This will stop the base being permanently damp and prevent the wood rotting too quickly. Line the base and sides of the crate with the plastic, making sure – if you're using a compost bag – the black side is outermost so you don't see garish colours through the slats of the box once planted. It doesn't matter if the plastic pokes up above the edges of the box at this point. With your scissors, make several drainage holes in the plastic over the base of the crate, preferably lining them up with the gaps in the wooden boards so drainage water has as little contact with the wood as possible.

Fill the lined crate almost to the top with compost then pick up the box and gently tap it a couple of times on the ground to help the compost settle. Add more compost if necessary so that the level is a couple of inches from the top. Now cut off any excess plastic with your scissors so you can't see it. Sprinkle the seeds on the surface of the compost so they are about 5cm apart, then gently cover them with compost by ruffling the surface with your fingers. Water well.

Once the seedlings have reached about 10cm high, thin them out to about 10cm apart, nipping out the growing shoot down to a strong pair of side buds. This encourages the plants to bush out strongly. As the cosmos grows, you may need to prop up the plants with some twigs. Keep watered and don't forget to deadhead – cutting the spent flower stems back to a flower bud or to a growing point. This way the plants won't become top heavy with old flowers and droop.

right Sow cosmos directly into your container to create a jungle of blooms, and keep deadheading to prolong flowering right up to the first frost.

R. MITCHELL (LONDON) LTD
COVENT GARDEN

A meadow in a cattle trough

Large containers such as cattle troughs, baths or tanks can be expensive to fill if you buy individual plants. One packet of seeds, however, costs hardly anything and these days you can buy some fantastic meadow mixes from garden centres or online that are designed for small spaces. They are usually a combination of poppies, ox-eye daisies, cornflowers and other common field annuals, which together will deliver maximum visual impact. Sow in spring and you'll have a gorgeous profusion of colour that will be a magnet for pollinating insects and bring a marvellous dash of exuberant wildness in even the most built-up of gardens, from summer right through to autumn. If you have several large containers, why not divide a packet between them?

The great thing about a meadow in a container is that you can mimic any type of soil you want, and hence control the type of wildflowers you end up with. Chalkland, for example, tends to support one of the most diverse range of wildflowers. You can mimic chalkland soil by adding a handful of garden lime to the compost, which makes it more alkaline. You can also buy seed appropriate for shady, acid-loving, sunny or even coastal conditions.

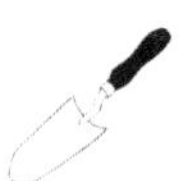

You will need

1 large container such as a cattle trough, old tin bath or pot with drainage holes
Drill or hammer and nail (optional)
Multipurpose, peat-free organic compost
Garden soil (if you don't have a garden, use seed compost since it is low in nutrients – wild flowers need a very poor soil to grow well)
Horticultural grit
1 packet of wildflower meadow mixed seeds – look on the internet for inspiration for a mix that suits you
Watering can with rose attachment

When to do it

Spring

How to do it

Position your container where you want it, bearing in mind that, once filled, it will probably be too heavy to move. Make sure it has sufficient drainage holes and if not make some with a drill or hammer and nail. Now mix up your multipurpose compost with garden soil and grit aiming for a ratio of 1:2:1. If you have no garden soil available, use seed compost and mix with grit at a ratio of 3:1.

Now simply scatter your seeds over the surface of the soil and water in well using a watering can with a rose attachment. Within a couple of weeks the seedlings will emerge and by midsummer the plants should start to flower. By late autumn, you can save seed from annual plants before clearing them (see page 110) or leave the seed heads on over winter, which can look quite sculptural. Perennial wildflower plants should be left in situ over their first winter. The following autumn – and every autumn after that – cut them to within 10cm of soil level.

By late autumn, after flowering, try saving the seed of annual flowers (see page 110) for sowing again next year. Perennial wild flowers will last several years.

A tapestry of succulents

Sempervivums, often called house leeks or hen and chicks, are charming, slow-growing, succulent plants that look perfect in pots, particularly as a centrepiece for a garden table where their small, prehistoric-looking rosettes can be fully appreciated. Purple, green, round, spiky – there are many types, but all multiply themselves by making plantlets that you can simply pull off and replant (see Taking Offsets, page 113). It couldn't be simpler. Sempervivums are also drought tolerant, so once you've given them an initial watering you won't have to worry about them. Their shallow roots and minimal irrigation demands make them ideal for shallow containers such as this picture frame.

This living painting will look striking all year round and makes a fantastic focal point for a wall in a small urban courtyard or balcony. You can pick up picture frames cheaply in charity or junk shops, and the rest of the materials can easily by sourced from home improvement stores.

You will need

1 picture frame (bear in mind, the bigger the frame, the heavier the finished tapestry will be)
1 wood saw
Timber baton to make the frame. The length depends on the size of the frame (see instructions below). For a large frame, choose a baton 5 x 3cm; for a smaller frame, 3 x 1cm.
1 tape measure
1 drill
1m² of greenhouse shading material (you can buy this by the metre from a home improvement store), or if you can't find this, use weed suppressing membrane
Exterior wood glue
Weights, such as bricks
1 bag sphagnum moss (the kind used for lining hanging baskets)
1 bag soil-based compost (such as John Innes No 2)
1 piece of exterior plywood to form the back of the frame (you can get this cut to measure at major DIY stores)
Scissors
Enough sempervivums (house leeks) to fill the frame, in various colours
Watering can with a rose attachment

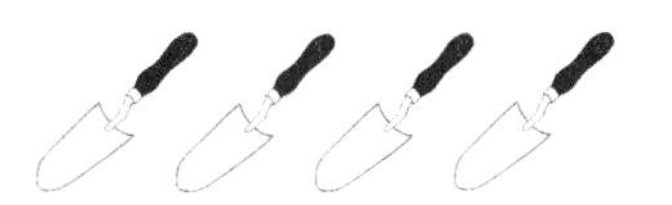

How to do it

Turn over the picture frame and lay it flat on the ground. With your saw, cut the timber baton into four pieces that fit along the four sides of the back of the frame to create a box. It makes sense to fit this box to the inner rather than outer edges of the frame to make the finished tapestry less heavy. Lay the narrower edge of the timber baton on the frame with the deeper edge vertical to give the box more depth for the plants to grow in it.

Next, take your piece of greenhouse shading material and lay it on the back of the picture frame. Pull it taut. It doesn't matter if it overhangs. Apply wood glue all around the edge of the frame onto the shading material and also onto the bottom sides of the four wooden batons. Stick these batons down on top of the shading material to create the box and weigh them down with something heavy (bricks, for example) until the surfaces bond securely. Allow to dry thoroughly. Now drill three holes in the bottom edge of the frame, each around 2mm in diameter. These will act as drainage holes so the compost does not become waterlogged.

Mix together the sphagnum moss and compost in equal quantities and then press it into the box. Tuck it into every corner and make sure the whole box is full, otherwise the compost will drop to the bottom when you stand the picture frame upright.

1. Cut your timber baton into 4 pieces to make a box that fits onto the back of the frame.
2. Glue the greenhouse shading onto the picture frame.
3. Stick the batons on top of the shading material to make a box.
4. Drill drainage holes in the bottom of the frame.
5. Mix moss and compost together and pour into the frame.
6. Cut plywood to fit the back of the frame.
7. With scissors, cut crosses in the shading material.
8. Push in your plants.

Once you are happy that it is filled, cut the piece of plywood to fit the box and glue it onto the batons. If you don't want to cut the plywood, most big DIY stores offer a cutting service when you buy from them. If you are hanging the picture on a wall, drill a hole in the top of the plywood to hang it from. Weigh down the plywood back with stones, plant pots or anything heavy to ensure the bond is secure.

Once the glue is dry and bonded, flip over the frame; you are now ready to plant. Using scissors, cut crosses in the shading material and push in your plants, aiming for a varied spread of colours and textures. The material will keep the plants and soil from falling out.

Try to fill the frame completely, but if you can still see some material, don't worry, the plants will soon grow to hide it. Water the frame from above with a watering can fitted with a rose attachment. Leave the frame lying flat on the ground for a week to let the plants settle and root into the compost, then mount it on a wall or prop it up on a ledge where it can be admired.

To care for your succulent tapestry, lay it flat every couple of weeks and water it. Leave to drain for half an hour or so before hanging it up again.

A cool colander of ferns

Hanging baskets are always useful, giving you much-needed planting options for small spaces like balconies and urban gardens. The traditional wicker or metal basket sold in garden centres, however, can look a little twee and old-fashioned. Using alternative containers updates the hanging basket idea, and colanders are particularly good since they already have handy handles to tie your string to (old metal buckets can look good too and are easily hung from their handles). Look out for old colanders in junk shops, boot fairs and on eBay and freecycle.

As long as you cover some of the drainage holes at the bottom to keep moisture in, colanders make very successful containers for many plants – from strawberries to salad, to violas to ferns. This trio of colanders planted with ferns will add interest and a cool, mellow atmosphere to a shady corner in the garden. Or hang them from a pergola over an outside dining table. Ferns like a moist soil, so lining the colanders with an old woollen jumper (failing that, a compost bag with holes in it) will keep the compost damp.

You will need

An old woollen jumper you don't want any more (or a compost bag with holes in it)
3 metal colanders
A soil-based compost such as John Innes No 2 or 3
3 ferns, such as eared lady fern (*Athyrium otophorum* 'Okanum'), hart's tongue fern (*Asplenium scolopendrium*) and common polypody (*Polypodium vulgare*)
Strong weatherproof string or cord, such as drapery cord, for hanging
Scissors

How to do it

Cut the woollen material to size and press it into the base of your colander, then top with a little compost. Position the ferns, fill around them with more compost, then water well. Cut your string or cord to the length you want and hang up the basket in a shady place. Hanging each basket at a slightly different length and grouping them in a cluster can look very effective. Make sure you water the ferns every few days and feed once a month (see page 145 for How to Make your Own Plant Feeds).

Give cheap plastic pots the sack

There's no getting away from it; when you're looking for a large container, by far the cheapest options are plastic. They make a lot of sense, too; they're hard wearing, light and – in the case of plastic garden pots – come with built-in drainage holes. You can buy them for a snip from garden centres or get free plastic buckets from delis or other food stores. Multicoloured tub trugs are also available from homewares stores and make great planters since they're so large and have handles for easy hauling.

However, plastic will always look unnatural and manmade and some of the colours available also require sunglasses. These containers will upstage your plants – and not in a good way. There is a cheap way to get these plastic pots to blend in, though. By wrapping the pot in a natural material such as hessian or burlap, you turn them from a garish manmade object to something far less conspicuous. Simply put the pot in the sack and tuck the material over the rim. The material will get stained and yucky after a year, but as a temporary, extremely cheap (even free) screen to plastic-not-so-fantastic, they're a neat solution.

If you're lucky you might be able to get sacks for free from your greengrocer. If not, hessian potato sacks are sold at a very reasonable price from garden suppliers. Coffee sacks are even better, since they are larger and can have attractive lettering on them. Try eBay for these.

A vintage, tin herb garden

Herbs are not only indispensable in the kitchen, but they often make very beautiful plants too. Free-flowering, aromatic and drought-tolerant, herbs are the perfect choice for small containers such as old tins. If you choose a variety of different shapes, colours and styles you can create a quirky mini garden with lots of charm. Most of us have some old tins hanging around but if not, ask your friends and relatives or keep your eye out in charity shops, on freecycle, jumble sales, boot fairs, junk stores and eBay for some bargains. Since you won't be using them to store food, it doesn't matter if they're rusty, dented, or even have holes. Vintage-style lettering and vibrant colours can look great in a garden, courtyard or balcony setting. Either group them together on the ground, line them up on a windowsill or hang them on a wall or from railings.

Go for herbs that stay relatively small rather than large, bushy ones such as rosemary and sage, and your herbs can stay in their tins for several years. Just make sure you pierce drainage holes in the bottom.

You will need

A variety of old tins
Drill or hammer and nail
Soil-based compost such as John Innes No 2
Horticultural grit or perlite
Compact herbs – including basil, thyme, oregano, marjoram, chives, mint, winter savory, coriander, chervil – one plant per tin

How to do it

Turn over your tins and make three to five holes in the base of each. Fill each three-quarters full with a 50:50 mix of compost and grit/perlite, then plant your herb. Water well and top dress with grit (or pea shingle if you have a driveway that can spare a bit). This not only makes the containers look smarter, but keeps moisture in the compost so you won't have to water as often.

Savvy Tip

Choose compact and annual herbs for smaller containers such as tea caddies. Larger woody herbs such as rosemary and sage are better planted in cake or biscuit tins. If making drainage holes with a nail, make sure the hole is large enough to let water out.

COLMAN'S MUSTARD
FLEXOLITE
LIGHTER FLUID CAPSULES
HIGHLY INFLAMMABLE
FLEXOLITE LTD CHELL STOKE-ON-TRENT ENGLAND
FLEXOLITE
FLEXOLITE
LIGHTER FLUID CAPSULES
LIGHTER FLUID CAPSULES

Style on a Shoestring

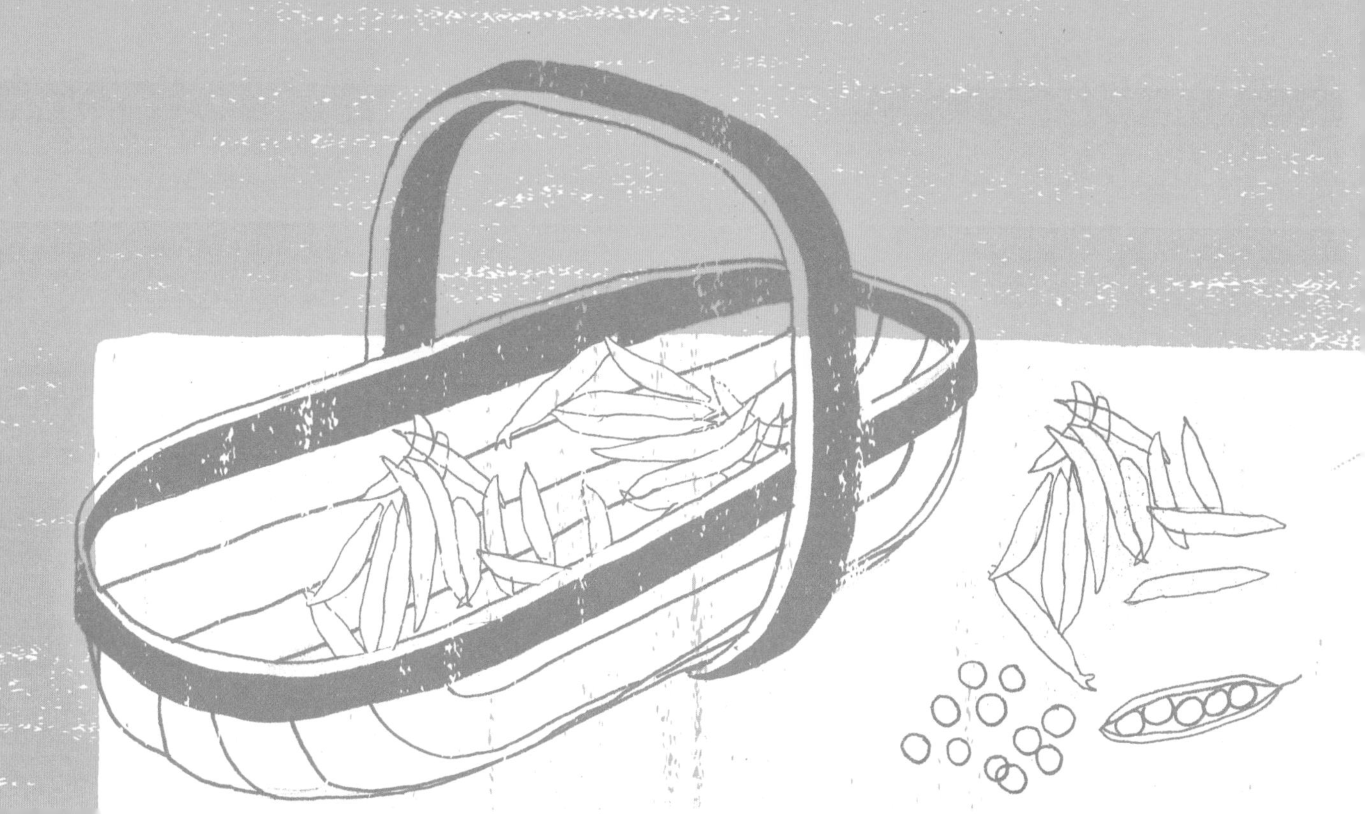

Gardening with a budget in mind doesn't mean you have to give up on style. Whether you want a family-friendly garden to kick a football around in, a romantic, informal cottage garden, a modern urban space with clean lines or a naturalistic prairie swaying with long grasses, you can achieve the look without having to dig deep in your pocket. Here are some ideas...

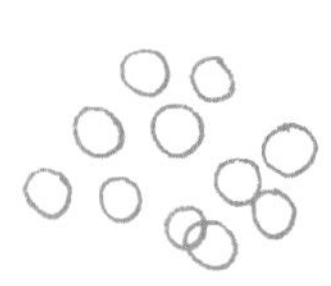

The cottage garden

Imagine a thatched cottage with a rose scrambling over the door, a picket fence and a wiggly brick path leading through jumbles of hollyhocks, sweet peas and love-in-the-mist. That's a cottage garden. In fact, that's the picture-book garden – romantic, informal, charming – and you don't have to live in a thatched cottage to achieve it. Although it wouldn't hurt…

This style of gardening has evolved from traditional workers' cottages of generations past, where limited funds and space meant fruit trees and vegetables rubbed shoulders with flowers and medicinal herbs, chickens pecked at snails in the borders and any hard materials used were local, handmade or recycled – and kept to a minimum. Paths were usually made from recycled bricks or loose gravel, and fences from bits of local wood or woven panels of willow. If garden furniture was needed, it was dragged outside from the house rather than left out all year.

This sort of garden is all about the plants – and there are lots of them. It doesn't matter what you grow, but cottage gardens should be colourful, busy and just a bit chaotic, packed with many different cheerful annuals, biennials and climbers. Traditionally plants were grown from seed and left to self-seed where they fell, resulting in a beautiful informality. There are no straight lines and no real rules in cottage gardening, so this style could not be more ideal for the budget-conscious gardener. There is a bare minimum of hard landscaping to fork out for either, leaving lots of space for plants that seed themselves, returning year after year at no cost and no effort.

Five tips to create a cottage garden on a shoestring

1. Keep hard landscaping to a minimum to leave lots of space for plants.

2. Garden furniture doesn't have to be neat and uniform; sling a tablecloth over any old table and use cheap mismatched wooden chairs. Avoid using plastic pots or furniture in this scheme; vintage troughs, crates and other recycled containers are ideal.

3. Grow hedges as boundaries instead of fences; a native mix of hawthorn, holly, field maple, hazel and beech bought as bare-root plants can be extremely cost effective and will give your garden an informal, rustic character and attract interesting wildlife.

4. Buy seed or collect it and take cuttings and divisions from your friends' gardens to start off your garden, rather than fork out for relatively expensive young plants. If you sow in mid-spring your borders will be beautiful orgy of colour by midsummer.

5. Don't mulch and be careful when weeding! Many classic cottage-garden plants spread by self-sowing and mulching can smother these seedlings. It's all too easy to pull up 'weeds' that are actually beautiful flowers-to-be, too. You'll soon learn to recognise the juvenile forms of your favourite plants so you can leave them where they are or move them to a better place, but until then, pause for thought before you pull!

How to plant a cottage garden: **design tips**

As everyone knows, it's not easy to make beautiful chaos. Even with a style as informal as cottage gardening, there are a few tips worth considering when planting up your borders.

Avoid planting in rows or geometric blocks. Instead, aim for a random-looking pattern (as if the plants have self-sown naturally). The only exception is down the side of paths, where a line of lavender, for example, can give some useful structure.

Punctuate a sea of flowers with taller specimens to add height and variation to a border. Grow climbers up willow or hazel wigwams made either from wood you have collected yourself or bought inexpensively. (See How to Make a Willow Wigwam, page 128.) Let several plants share one support: runner beans, morning glory and clematis could all be grown up one wigwam.

Let plants self-seed in cracks in paving or brick paths. Generally, it's a good idea to place taller plants at the back and lower-growing ones nearer the front of the border, but breaking this rule now and then will make your planting look more exciting and spontaneous.

above Japanese anemones add height to a colourful jumble and edges are blurred with oregano and creeping thyme.

Get the look: 17 cottage-garden must-haves

Sun-Lovers

Hollyhocks *above centre*

With their lofty towers clothed in individual flowers as big as saucers, white or pink hollyhocks will live for several years if they are happy.

Make more plants by: saving seed, page 110.

Delphiniums

Exclamation marks of deepest blue, lavender or purple. Grow the stunning sky-blue 'Summer Skies' from seed.

Make more plants by: saving seed, page 110.

Sweet peas

Probably the definitive scent of summer. Keep cutting these and they will keep on blooming. Don't let the plants dry out as they are susceptible to powdery mildew when stressed.

Make more plants by: saving seed, page 110.

Mexican Fleabane (*Erigeron karvinskianus*) *above left*

With its habit of self-seeding in cracks in paving and along the edge of walls, this low mat-forming daisy is an essential for an informal cottage garden look. The small daisy flowers start off white then turn pink with yellow middles so the effect en masse is two-tone exuberance. Bees and butterflies love it too. Plant it once and you'll soon have it everywhere.

Make more plants by: saving seed, page 110.

Love-in-a-mist (*Nigella damascena*)

A delicate filigree of tendrils surrounds these exquisite blue flowers. Once you've grown nigella you'll always have it, since it self-seeds everywhere, appearing in cracks in paths and paving too.

Make more plants by: saving seed/transplanting self-sown seedlings, page 110/112.

Phlox (*Phlox paniculata*)

A cheerful cottage-garden favourite that's chock-a-block with bright pink flowers and has the added bonus of a heady scent.

Make more plants by: taking root cuttings, page 114.

Oregano (*Origanum vulgare*) *above right*

Yes, it's technically a culinary herb, but allow this frothy carpet of fresh green and white into your garden and you won't regret it. Bees flock to the flowers and it will self-seed everywhere, filling gaps and giving your cottage garden an air of charming, scented spontaneity.

Make more plants by: transplanting self-sown seedlings, page 112.

Cosmos

Like daisies on steroids, these large-flowered biddable annuals will bloom their hearts out all summer long until the first frosts if you keep deadheading them. *Cosmos bipinnatus* 'Sensation Mixed' is the one to go for. One packet sown direct into the soil in spring will produce a cloud of tall pink, white and carmine flowers within a month or so.

Make more plants by: saving seed, page 110.

***Rudbeckia* 'Marmalade'**

With flowers like the heads of smiley cartoon lions, this is a plant with unfailing cheer. It makes a magnificent cut flower too.

Make more plants by: saving seed, page 110.

Oriental poppy (*Papaver orientale*)

With their magnificent crumpled tissue-paper petals and black pepperpot centres, oriental poppies are big, blowsy and over-the-top. Who cares that the flowers only last a few days when there are so many of them? Oriental poppies spread by underground runners so if you have a friend with an established patch – whether orangey pillarbox red or the dusky pink shot silk of 'Patty's Plum' – get in there with your fork and get yourself a few.

Make more plants by: taking root cuttings, page 114.

***Calendula officinalis* 'Indian Prince'**

Another yellow cheerer-upper, this will grow even in very poor soil and is pretty drought tolerant too. Zingy orange and fresh green leaves make this a traditionally vivid addition to the vegetable garden, where it attracts pollinating insects. It looks great in pots too. You can also eat the petals in salads (they don't taste of much but they look lovely).

Make more plants by: saving seed, page 110.

Michaelmas daisies (*Aster*) *above centre*

Just when you think it's all over in the garden in late summer, these little colourful daisies take up the baton and see you through to autumn on a tide of colour. Go for the New England group (check the label) if you want to avoid mildew. If you only have room for one, make it *Aster novae-angliae* 'September Ruby', which has a profusion of stunning, deep reddish-pink flowers.

Make more plants by: division, page 117.

Shade-lovers

Flowering tobacco (*Nicotiana sylvestris*) *above left*

No shady garden should be without the lofty white umbrellas of the flowering tobacco, with their musky scent of summer.

Make more plants by: saving seed, page 110.

Foxglove (*Digitalis purpurea*)

These irresistible towering spires bring a dash drama to any garden. The flowering spikes shoot up to over a metre tall and are fantastic at the back of a border or anywhere in dappled shade.

Make more plants by: transplanting self-sown seedlings, page 112.

Granny's bonnet (*Aquilegia vulgaris*)

This beautiful plant has flowers with long spurs that seem to dance above delicate stems. Give them partial shade and they will be happy.

Make more plants by: saving seed, page 110.

Honesty (*Lunaria annua*)

It would be worth growing this lovely woodland plant for its seed heads alone, green discs turning to delicate translucent rice paper by midsummer. The delightful mauve or white flowers clinch the deal. Wonderful in shady spots .

Make more plants by: saving seed, page 110.

Dusky cranesbill (*Geranium phaeum*) *above right*

This is one of the most delicate and exquisite geraniums, with small burgundy flowers above leaves splotched with chocolate. It thrives in shade but is also happy in sun, will fill gaps, hide bare earth and generally just get on with it.

Make more plants by: division, p117.

Making a border

Location

First think about where you want your border to be. Sunny or shady, there are plants for pretty much every spot, though the most difficult location is under large trees. These areas are not only shady but also extremely dry, since the tree roots take all the moisture out of the earth, so avoid these if you can.

Shape and size

Now consider the shape. If your garden is long and thin, making a long strip of border either side will accentuate this. If you want to make your garden seem wider and longer, consider curved borders, as these prevent the eye seeing all the way down to the end. One large flower border can make a garden look lopsided so consider balancing it the other side with another border.

Now consider how wide your border will be. Anything narrower than 1m will look fairly weedy, so aim for wider than this if you can.

Marking out

Once you have decided on the shape and location of your border, mark out the edge. If you have some sand available, fill a plastic water bottle with it, make a hole in the lid and sprinkle the sand to define the edge you want. If not, spray line paint works well or, if it's a curved bed, a garden hose laid flat. Then carefully push down along this line with a garden spade to define a clear edge.

Get digging

If the area is already planted up, simply start digging with a fork. Tackle a couple of square metres at a time rather than the whole area and dig to a fork's depth. Remove stones, weeds and roots, and break up the soil with the back of the fork to make it crumbly.

If you are turning lawn into a border, take a spade and push it horizontally under the turf to remove the grass in sections. Stack these turves, grass-side down, in a corner of the garden. In time they will break down into lovely fertile compost.

As you dig, have a look at the soil. If it is dark brown, crumbly and digs easily, it is a regular loam. This is the best sort of soil for planting in and you can plant straight away without improving it. If it is very sodden with lichen and algae on the surface, you know it's a wet soil with poor drainage. If it is very dusty, you know it is dry and probably low in nutrients. If it is sticky and relatively pale in colour, it is a clay soil, so heavy to work. To get an even clearer sense of your soil, repeat the handful test from page 9.

Improve your soil...within reason

Any soil can be altered to some extent with the addition of organic matter and/or grit to improve drainage and fertility. However, if your soil is naturally heavy you would be wise to stick to plants that thrive in these conditions. A Mediterranean collection of drought-tolerant plants is likely to suffer in sticky clay conditions, but will thrive in sandy, light soils in which water runs through the soil quickly. Check the plant label before you buy. Work with what you have and your plants are likely to be healthy and happy.

Whatever soil you have, adding well rotted organic matter in the shape of garden compost, farmyard compost or spent mushroom compost will give it a boost, improving drainage and adding nutrients. If you don't already have a functioning compost bin on the go (see page 139) try contacting your local authority to see if you can buy recycled green waste compost for a very reasonable price. If you live in a rural spot, find out if there is a mushroom farm nearby – the compost they grow the mushrooms in is a waste product of this industry and a great soil conditioner. Spread a 10cm layer of organic matter on the surface of the soil and dig it in loosely with your fork.

Playing with shapes

Now you are ready to get planting. Autumn and spring are best, since these are the seasons for sowing and the times when garden centres have most plants available. When it comes to choosing plants, try not to get too distracted by flower colours and think of the plants in terms of shapes.

Stand in the spot in which you would want to view the border and draw shapes in the air with your finger. Do you want a big mass in one spot? Tall spikes somewhere else, and something low elsewhere? Large-leaved drama or fluff? If you have a big round shape on one side, balance it out on the other with a similar shape.

Once you have worked out the shapes, think about how the border will look in winter – unless you include some evergreen plants it will

Dense, rounded shapes for presence all year

Box
Bay
Viburnum
Pittosporum
Euphorbia characias
Santolina
Lavender

Towering spikes

for sun . . .
Culver's root
Foxtail lily
Verbascum
Delphiniums
Penstemons

for shade . . .
Foxgloves
Actaea racemosa

Cloudy fluff to knit plants together

Ammi majus
Orlaya grandiflora
Hardy geraniums
Asters
Catmint

Wispy shapes

Ornamental grasses
Fennel

Large-leaved drama

Fatsia japonica
Melianthus major
Phormiums
Ferns

Low-growing plants for the front of the border

Bergenia
Lady's mantle
Lamb's ears

be bare for much of the year. Remember, in principle, taller things should go at the back, but breaking this up occasionally can be dynamic. Remember, too, that the eye likes a pattern and repeating groups of the same plant along the length of the border can look very harmonious and draw the eye along.

Unless they are very large, plants should be placed in groups of threes, fives or sevens. Dotting them singly around the place will look like a hotch potch – the eye cannot take in random dots, so it will look like a mess. Planting in groups gives a sense of rhythm and lets the eye register the various shapes and colours much more comfortably.

What plants?

Once you have worked out the shapes you want, you can work out which plants will fit them. Plants are your tools to achieve the effect you want. Bear in mind the soil you have and try to match the plant to these conditions. Keep your eyes open when you're walking down the street or visiting friends and relatives' gardens, and pop your head over the garden fence to get ideas.

Colour

Obviously you cannot neglect colour entirely, but in borders restraint is the key to success. Aim for no more than four or five colours, and remember white is a colour too. If you are aiming for an 'all white' border, remember that cream and white are different and don't always look right together.

Remember, too, that green is not just green. Acid greens such as that of lady's mantle can look really striking next to the dark green of box.

Buying your plants

Now buy your plants. If you're lucky, you will be able to get lots of free plants from your friends (see How to Make New Plants for Free, page 108). Depending on the time of year, some plants can be sown directly into the border or into small pots for planting out later. Others you will have to buy.

To save money aim for smaller specimens of plants. These are often far cheaper and will soon catch up with larger ones.

How to make a sweet pea tunnel

Arches and pergolas add useful height to any garden scheme, but they can be expensive to buy. Why not make your own structure over a path for a cottage-garden vibe? It's easier than you'd think and the tunnel can be as long as you like. This tunnel creates a fun approach to a kids' trampoline. Simply buy some willow rods and sweet pea seeds and within a couple of months you will have a beautiful scented walkway.

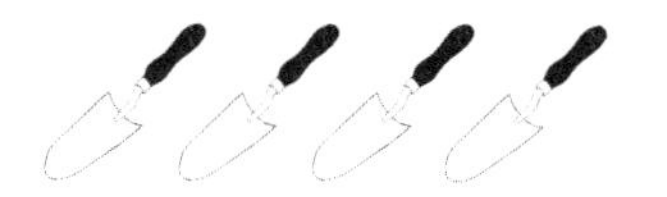

You will need

Brown, soaked willow rods (not living or green, since this may root). For every metre of tunnel you will need around 40 rods each about 3m long (if the tunnel is for children they could be 2.5m). See page 126 for more advice on sourcing willow.
Garden twine
Scissors
Sweet pea seeds

When to do it

Any time for the structure; sow sweet pea seeds in spring

How to do it

Push the thick end of the rods into the ground on either side of the path, spacing them more or less equally, at a distance of about 8cm apart. Now bend over the tops of each opposing pair so they meet in the middle. When you are happy with the height of the tunnel, tie the rods together at that point to form a series of arches. Strengthen the top of the tunnel by twirling any thin ends left over around the opposite rod and tying in the ends securely.

Now strengthen the sides of the tunnel and give your sweet peas plenty of horizontal supports to climb. Make sure the rods have been soaked (see page 126) so they are sufficiently flexible. Take a rod and carefully weave it horizontally through all the uprights, about 20cm from the ground. If it doesn't reach all the way to the end of the tunnel, continue with a new rod, tying in any loose ends as you go. Repeat just above the first lateral, but this time weaving in the alternate pattern to create a strong bond. Weave in a further rod so you have three laterals and then repeat this on the other side of the tunnel. Weave in two further groups of laterals on each side, at about 40cm intervals, so that the tunnel feels strong and secure.

Now you are ready to sow your sweet peas. Space seeds about 5cm apart along the base of the tunnel on each side. You want a profusion of colour, so really pack in the seeds. Water well and protect the seedlings from slugs and snails until they are established. Tie in the stems to the supports as they grow to help them along and when they start flowering, keep picking to encourage them to produce more blooms. Don't allow any seedpods to form apart from on those plants you are growing in order to save their seeds.

Make your willow tunnel any length you like and sow your sweetpeas densely to maximise colour and scent as you walk through.

The modern garden

Defined by clean lines and a restrained palette of colours and materials, a modern garden has a relatively formal feel. In this style of garden there is more hard landscaping in proportion to plants than you would find with a traditional look, but those plants that are there tend to be carefully chosen statement specimens, selected for their sculptural forms or magnificent foliage. Low-maintenance and year-round structure are key here, so there tends to be a lot of evergreen plants – often topiarised into spheres and other formal shapes. The planting is often predominantly green, although frequently punctuated with white and almost-black flowers and tends to accentuate the lines of the garden, with rows of lavender, for example, lining the edges of a straight path. The overall effect is stylish, understated and expensive. So how can you create a garden like this on a budget?

left and above Pots of sculptural succulents placed each side of garden steps bring a sense of symmetry; sculpture strikes a contemporary tone. **right** The striking serrated foliage of honey bush (*Melianthus major*).

How to plant a modern garden: **style tips**

Save your money for a handful of impressive sculptural plants that you love and place these in prominent positions or as focal points at the end of the garden. Fill in the gaps with inexpensive groundcover plants to keep costs down.

Plant to accentuate the symmetry and lines of the garden. Edge a straight path with repeats of the same plant to encourage the eye to travel along its length – box balls are always good, perhaps interspersed with lavender (*Lavandula angustifolia* 'Hidcote') or catmint (*Nepeta* 'Six Hills Giant'). Flank doorways or the entrance to a path with a pair of identical pots or plants.

Keep the variety of the plants restrained. A combination of three or four different plants may be all you need in a small garden. A simple mix of white foxgloves (*Digitalis purpurea* 'Alba') with lady's mantle and box, for example, can be elegant and effective.

Clothe walls and fences with evergreens such as wall-trained camellias and climbing hydrangea for a handsome, restful backdrop against which statement plants can be allowed to shine. These will give good structure even over winter.

Get the look: 10 modern garden must-haves

Inexpensive groundcover plants

Lady's mantle (*Alchemilla mollis*)

Acid-green scallop leaves that catch droplets of rain and a froth of tiny flowers give this common garden plant an architectural quality that fits in perfectly in a modern-style garden. Most people have this in their gardens and it's a prolific self-seeder, so pay a visit to someone who has it and see if you can hoik out a few seedlings to start off with.

Make more plants by: transplanting self-sown seedlings, page 112.

Wild ginger (*Asarum europaeum*)

Evergreen kidney-shaped leaves that make a glossy carpet – great for a shady spot. This plant spreads quickly, especially if planted in fertile soil, so buy small plants and add lots of compost.

Make more plants by: division, page 117.

Buy alliums as bulbs rather than plants to keep costs down. Start with only a few bulbs and then once a clump has become established you can divide it in spring or autumn to increase your collection.

Wow-factor statement plants

Honey bush (*Melianthus major*)

With arching, serrated, grey-green leaves that smell of peanut butter, this tropical-looking shrub is a real conversation point. If you're lucky you'll also get tall, magenta flowering spikes. It's surprisingly hardy too. Not an inexpensive plant, but worth every penny.

Olive trees (*Olea europaea*)

An aged olive tree instantly gives a garden gravitas, but even small, young trees are objects of beauty and surprisingly inexpensive. Just make sure you buy a variety that will survive your climate. Three potted olive trees in a row makes a strong statement.

Japanese maples (*Acers*)

Acers have such elegant foliage and striking sculptural shapes that they add instant interest to any garden. They tend to be slow growing so are ideal for small gardens and containers. Grow them in pots in a shady spot at the end of a path and sit back and watch the leaves change colour throughout the seasons like natural fireworks. The snakebark maple (*Acer davidii 'George Forrest'*) has particularly yellow-orange leaves in autumn and striped bark, while *Acer griseum* has shaggy bark and red foliage.

Grasses

The tidier, more compact ornamental grasses give useful year-round structure and also bring in movement with their wavy stems. They're ideal for the low-maintenance gardener since most require nothing more than a chop to the ground in early spring. *Miscanthus sinensis* 'Morning Light' has beautiful arching, silvery stems with a sculptural quality and *Imperata cylindrica* 'Rubra' has stunning scarlet-tipped leaves that give it its common name of Japanese blood grass.

Make more plants by: transplanting self-sown seedlings/division, page 112/117.

Bear's breeches (*Acanthus mollis* **or** *Acanthus Spinosa*)

Handsome dark glossy leaves and tall spikes covered with white flowers and purple bracts make this a striking addition to any shady garden. Redolent of Victoriana and grand houses, its strong form also lends itself to a modern garden.

Make more plants by: taking root cuttings, page 114.

Alliums

Basically a rod-straight stem with a lollipop flower on top, alliums are stylish punctuation marks to dot throughout your garden, plant en masse or pack densely into a large pot for a stunning focal point. *Allium hollandicum* 'Purple Sensation' is a classic purple globe while *A. cristophii* is topped by an enormous, effervescent ball of stars. For something more naturalistic though just as sculptural, try Sicilian honey garlic *(Nectaroscordum siculum),* which has achingly lovely drooping flowers with a subtle rose and cream colouring.

Make more plants by: division, page 117.

Black bamboo (*Phyllostachys nigra*)

Sophisticated purple-black stems and glossy dark green leaves make this one of the most elegant plants for the modern garden. Plant it en masse by the side of a path or in large containers where you can hear the leaves rustle in the breeze for a restful atmosphere. Great for screening ugly areas or lining awkward narrow spaces. Plants can be pricey, so you might like to start with a couple and then make new plants from them after a couple of years.

Make more plants by: division, page 117.

Australian tree ferns (*Dicksonia antarctica)*

With their prehistoric looking trunks and spectacular crown of fresh, green fronds, these giant ferns make impressive focal points for a modern garden, particularly if you are trying to convey an exotic feel. The only trouble is that they are expensive, mainly because they are so slow growing – those trunks take years to build up so you are paying for all that time they have spent in the nursery. If you are lucky enough to have a friend with a very mature tree fern with offsets growing around the base, you could take one of these and grow it on. But for most of us it's a question of either buying juvenile plants and being prepared to wait for the distinctive shaggy trunk to develop, or timing your purchase for end of season sales in the autumn when considerable discounts can be yours.

Make more plants by: taking offsets, page 113.

Above The architectural shapes of bear's breeches, left, are great planted in clumps at the back of a border or either side of an entrance. The delicate frondy leaves of *Acer dissectum* 'Purpureum', centre, look exotic and are particularly striking in their purple autumn colours. Drumstick alliums, right, provide dramatic punctuation marks in a contemporary garden.

Topiary on a shoestring

Most modern gardens feature some sort of evergreen topiary; whether it's box spheres or a potted standard bay tree with its top clipped into a ball. Evergreen bushes such as these are the bones of the garden over winter when many other plants have died back until spring. Topiary plants are surprisingly low maintenance – requiring only a trim in midsummer – and bring an instant air of formality and grandeur to a garden, however small.

Ready-trained box spheres are expensive because buxus is a slow-growing plant. You can save a lot of money if you buy bare-root box plants from hedging suppliers – look online for deals. Simply plant these and train them yourself, by snipping them into ball shapes. It will take several years to achieve this, but not only is it extremely satisfying to do, you'll be able to prune them into the shape you want. You also won't run the risk of an expensive mature topiarised shrub dying because you forgot to water it a week after planting...

Savvy Tip

For an even more cost-effective way to recreate the effect of topiarised box, try using a different plant altogether. *Ilex crenata*, or Japanese holly, looks almost identical to box and can be pruned in just the same way, but tends to be more affordable and won't suffer from box blight – a disease that can wipe out plants in an instant.

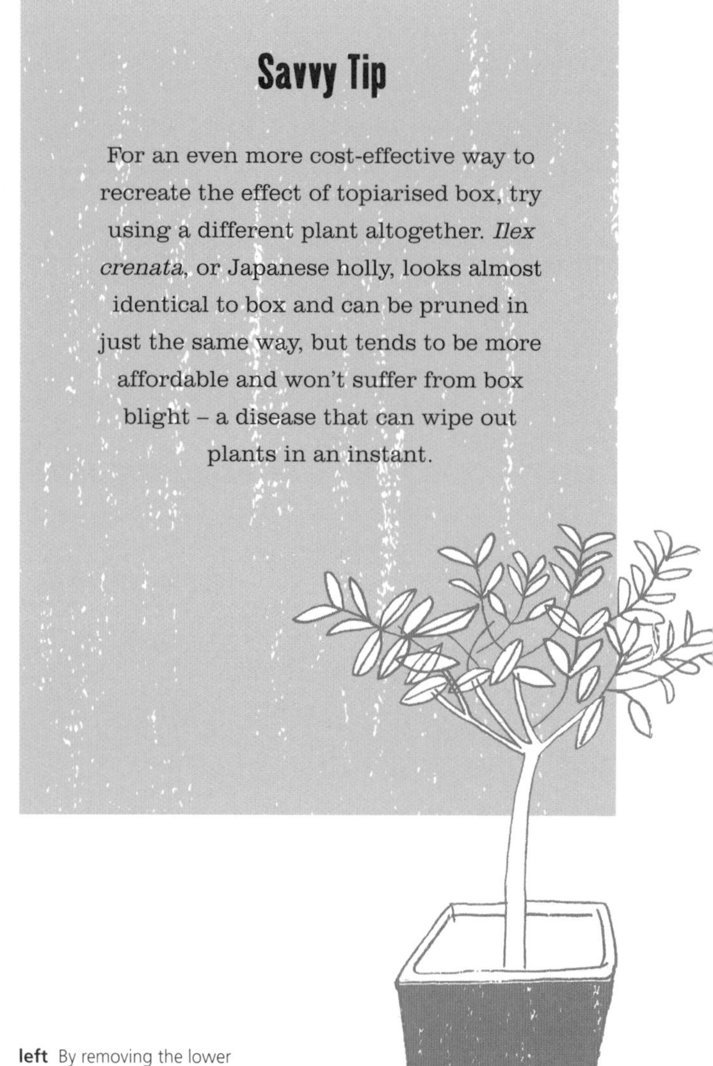

left By removing the lower branches, this bay was transformed from a messy overgrown blob to an elegant topiarised tree.

To create a standard bay tree – the classic lollipop tree beloved of the doorways of Italian trattorias – simply buy an untrained shrub and snip off most of the shoots along the main stem to leave just a handful of stems at the top to develop into a ball shape. Trim it twice a year to keep it in shape and encourage it to bush out.

Modern paving on a shoestring

An expanse of cool paving is a signature of a modern garden. Straight lines, formality and symmetry are key. Curvy paths that meander through billowy borders say cottage garden; a straight central path flanked by low box hedging heading towards a potted acer tree says modern. But stone paving can be eye-wateringly expensive.

If you are paving a small area – for dining, say, with a path – don't rule out buying new York stone. It may be expensive per unit, but laid en masse it could be worth the price for the beautiful flooring you will end up with. Shop around for deals. Alternatively, use Indian sandstone, which is far less expensive and, if you go for one of the styles that aims to mimic York stone, such as Antique York Grey, chances are no one will be able to tell the difference. Be aware, though, that there are many who disapprove of the sustainability of this sandstone, because it is shipped in from so far away.

To achieve a modern look, choose paving stones with sharp edges so the joints will be neat and straight. You want to keep the appearance of the hard landscaping as clean as possible, so go for relatively large slabs – even in small gardens – since this creates fewer distracting jointing lines.

Savvy tip

Many urban gardens contain areas of old, ugly concrete – whether paths or patio areas. The cost of breaking up and removing concrete is surprisingly high so it makes sense to leave it in situ. You can hide it completely, though, if you lay paving stones on top. If the thickness of paving stones will raise the level too much, use tiles instead, which are much thinner – as long as the concrete is basically sound, you can lay these on a layer of mortar or a resin bonding adhesive.

Modern pots on a shoestring

A stylish potted tree deserves a stylish pot. Classic terracotta is a failsafe material, but there's no need to buy an expensive pot, simply go for a large, factory-made pot and give it an aged look using the instructions on page 28.

Metal or fibre clay planters designed to look like lead also fit in well in a modern garden. Whatever material you choose, try to keep the look uniform – a mishmash of different types of stone or pot will spoil the harmonious, clean effect you're trying to achieve. And go for fewer larger pots rather than an eclectic jumble of small ones.

When planting up modern pots, keep it simple. One variety of plant en masse in a large container at the end of a path or on either side of a door will really catch the eye.

When considering plants, think beyond the usual suspects for those with interesting foliage and form. Aeoniums, for example, make for an eye-catching, dramatic window box. These prehistoric-looking succulents look rare and expensive, but if you buy just a couple – one green and one purple, for example – you can quite quickly build up a beautiful collection (see Stem Cuttings on page 116 for how to propagate them). Bring aeoniums inside over winter to keep them frost free.

Tulips, particualrly when restricted to one or two varietites, can look very effective in pots. To avoid having to buy new bulbs each year and make room in the pot for a follow-on display, remove the bulbs from the pot and plant into the ground as soon as they finish flowering. Remove the dead flower heads but not the leaves, then plant the bulbs back in the pot in autumn.

The family garden

This type of garden doesn't have to be all things to all people, it just has to provide something for everyone. That might mean leaving a football area of lawn and a trampoline for the kids while providing areas for grown ups such as a vegetable patch, a place for lounging in the sun and a decent-sized dining and barbecuing spot.

Shoestring ways to divide up a garden

Dividing the garden into sections is an ideal way to create spaces for everyone, and the average urban garden – which is usually relatively long and thin – responds well to this sort of treatment. A dining area surrounded by beautiful planting near the house can easily be separated from a lawn by a hedge or climbers, behind which footballs can be safely kicked. This creates a more peaceful environment for families – you can position your most precious, fragile plants for the area where you'll see them most and won't have to shout at the children every time they charge outside and threaten to damage them with their games.

Splitting up a long garden this way conversely makes it appear larger, since there is always the promise of more behind the screen. Make sure you leave gaps in the hedge – one in the middle and perhaps a couple either end too – which not only allows access but also offers a tantalising glimpse of what lies beyond.

Hedges

A fairly low – around 1.5m tall – neatly clipped hedge is probably the simplest, most affordable way to divide a garden. Good plants for this sort of boundary include evergreen yew – which has an undeserved reputation for being slow-growing – hornbeam or beech, which gives you lovely fresh green growth in summer and toasty brown leaves all winter.

When planting a hedge, time it for the bare-root season – which runs from winter to early spring – because bare-root plants cost much less than pot-grown specimens. Prepare the planting trench well, breaking up compact ground and removing weeds, and plant a double row of plants for a thick hedge. Don't forget to water the plants regularly in the first year.

Savvy tip

When buying hedging plants, take advantage of bare-root offers at the end of the planting season. These tend to come up towards the end of winter when nurseries are trying to get rid of their bare-root stock. Time it right and you could snap up a hedge for a small pittance.

Trellis

Climbers grown up a trellis can quickly screen an area of the garden by covering the structure and creating a green or flowering wall. Trellis panels are inexpensive to buy and if you paint them dark grey they won't appear so prominent. If making a freestanding trellis screen, make sure you attach it to strong posts in the ground.

left Dividing a long, thin family garden means that everyone can have their own area.
above right Clematis will cover a trellis fast and is easy to maintain.

Three climbers that will cover a trellis fast:

1. *Trachelospermum jasminoides* – evergreen, sweetly smelling, twining climber with dainty white flowers. Trim it back close to the trellis in spring if you want it to grow neatly.

2. *Solanum laxum 'Album'* – rampant white-flowered vine. Prune it in spring.

3. Clematis – any variety will clamber beautifully up a trellis; from the giant purple saucers of *Clematis 'Jackmanii'* to the profuse white charms of *Clematis montana* or the fragrance of evergreen *Clematis armandii*, there is a clematis for pretty much any spot and any garden.

How to screen a trampoline

Trampolines are ubiquitous nowadays. You can't avoid them, but you can at least try to conceal them. Some people sink their trampolines into a hole in the ground, but this is expensive and, unless it's done very carefully, can even be dangerous, with the potential for creating a sump of water and a gap through which children can fall. It is also rather debatable whether it's worth doing, since you need to have a protective net around the trampoline anyway and it's impossible to hide that.

Chances are, if you have a trampoline you have children who are too young to bounce on it entirely unwatched, so you need to screen it off without completely obscuring it. But just because you have to see the children doesn't mean you have to see the ugly metal frame. There's no need to stump up on a fence, if you choose the right plants you could be looking at waving grasses not metal bolts.

Try screening the trampoline with tall grasses such as *Stipa gigantea*, the flowering spikes of which can reach a staggering 2m high. Another great screening grass is *Calamagrostis x acutiflora* 'Karl Foerster', which forms a narrow umbrella stand of stems almost 2m high. Plant these close together and you'll make a beautiful natural fence that changes colour from pale green in summer to toasty brown through autumn and winter until you cut it to the ground in spring to start all over again. Intersperse these grasses with tall, see-through flowering plants such as purple globe thistle *(Echinops ritro)*, yellow-flowered bronze fennel, purple *Verbena bonariensis* and cerise *Cirsium rivulare* 'Atropurpureum' for a beautiful distraction.

Alternatively, plant a willow screen by rooting rods of living willow in a line in front of the trampoline or, for a delicious, fragrant summer screen, why not grow some sweet peas? A few bamboo canes with chicken wire strung in between them to form a circular structure would make a perfect climbing frame for morning glory or clambering nasturtiums too. Or just plant a lovely simple beech hedge and keep the top trimmed to just below bouncing height.

left Tall grasses and globe thistles
above right *Verbena bonariensis* soften the view of a large trampoline.

Lawns

If you're starting a lawn from scratch it's tempting to buy turf, but you'll save yourself a lot of money if you start it from seed instead. The work that must go into levelling and preparing the soil before laying it to lawn is pretty much identical whether you're turfing or sowing it, but the cost of seed is considerably less. Turf requires vigilance once it has been laid, since it is susceptible to drying out. Seed, on the other hand – if laid in spring or autumn when it isn't too dry – tends to be less demanding. Yes, seed takes longer to look decent – about two months before it looks like a proper lawn – but after that you won't know the difference.

Get the look: 10 football-friendly plants

You wouldn't want to stop your kids kicking or throwing balls around or having sword fights on the lawn, so why not plant things that won't mind the odd bash and thump?

1. Ornamental grasses will sway and bend but usually bounce back if bashed.

2. Box is so dense it will repel most ball invasions.

3. Roses – not ball-proof per se, but so thorny that a ball is unlikely to be deliberately hit in that direction twice.

4. *Euphorbia myrsinites* – springy and dense, this mat-forming evergreen will shrug off assault.

5. *Salvia nemorosa* 'Caradonna' – a beautiful mauve-flowering plant with upright spikey flowers that will bend not snap and a dense, tough cushion of leaves.

6. Catmint (*Nepeta*), with its lanky purple-flowering stems, has such a loose, sprawling habit that an incoming ball won't make much difference to its shape.

7. Lavender has surprisingly tough branches and will fight off most flying attacks.

8. Rosemary won't even notice a ball.

9. Thyme is a tough customer. In its native habitat this herb is trodden on and grazed by animals – a football is small fry.

10. Lady's mantle (*Alchemilla mollis*) is great for groundcover and forms a mat that will soon recover if squashed a bit.

clockwise, from top left: lavender, thyme, catmint and *Euphorbia myrsinites*.

How to make a kids' den from living willow

Children love a playhouse, but wooden ones tend to be pricey or difficult to build. You can make a fantastic circular structure from living willow for a fraction of the price with the added benefit that it will blend in naturally in the garden.

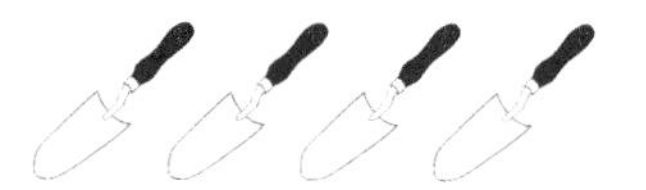

You will need

1 bundle of 3m-long living or green willow rods – hybrid varieties tend to be more disease resistant so are ideal. A typical-sized den would require around 45 rods. See page 126 for more advice on sourcing willow
1 long-handled screwdriver
Garden twine
Flexible plastic tie (such as Flexitie) (optional)
2 sticks or pegs
Scissors
Secateurs
Spade
Bark chips (optional)

When to do it

From mid-winter to early spring

How to do it

Choose a suitable site, avoiding anywhere on hard standing. Lawn is ideal. To mark out the base of your den, cut a piece of twine a little longer then the radius of the circle you want. Tie a stick to each end, push one stick into the ground at the centre and scratch out a circle in the turf with the other stick.

Grass will compete with the willow so it's best to plant it into bare earth. Strip all the turf inside the circle by pushing your spade horizontally just under the grass and removing it in sections. Stack these upside down somewhere – they'll rot down eventually into compost. If you want to have grass inside the den, remove only a 30cm-wide strip around the outer edge into which to plant the willow. If you choose this method, make sure you leave 1-metre of grass intact where you want the doorway to the den to be.

Snip the thicker end of each rod diagonally to make planting easier. Decide where you want your doorway to be and push two rods into the ground, to a depth of at least 15cm, close together to form one side of the door. Use the screwdriver to make the hole if it is difficult. Continue around the circle, pushing single rods into the ground every 20cm. When you reach the other side of the doorway push in two more rods close together to make the other doorpost. If you have removed all the turf inside the den, scatter some bark chips to make a soft, child-friendly floor and deter weeds.

To make the doorway, twist each pair of rods around each other and towards each other to make an arch. Twist the ends around and tie to secure. Make sure the arch is high enough to access easily.

To make the dome shape of the den, take opposite rods and bend them towards each other, twining the ends around each other to make it neat. Tie to secure. Now push more rods into the ground at a 45 degree angle either side of each of the uprights and weave them through the structure diagonally upwards to make a lattice pattern. Weave in the whippy ends and tie them off.

Keep the willow well watered until it is established. As your den sprouts leaves and grow, simply weave in any shoots that stick out to keep the dome shape tidy.

Savvy Tip

If you have a mature tree in the garden, pick up a free tyre from a tyre repair workshop. Spray-paint it with rubber paint and hang it up securely with rope.

above Flexible plastic ties secure the woven rods inconspicuously. Weave diagonal rods through the uprights to make a lattice.

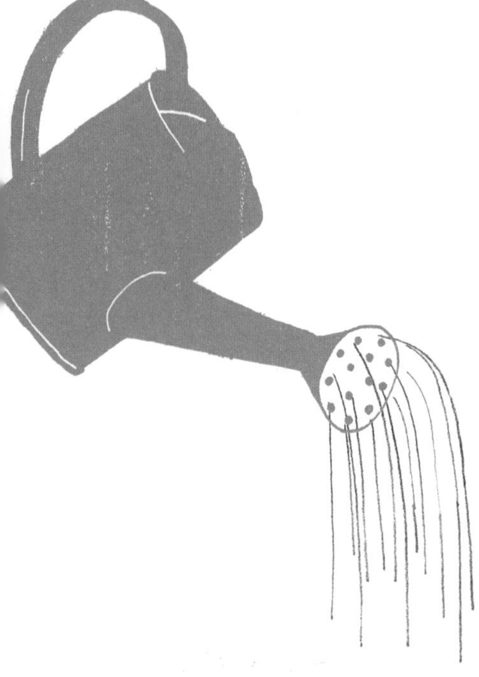

Grow their own

If you are growing fruit and vegetables in raised beds, give the children a bed for themselves. They're much more likely to get out there if they're doing their own thing rather than just helping you.

It's really easy to make an instant, no-dig mini raised bed if you have a few bricks lying around. Simply lay them out to create the edge of the bed and stack them two high. Place a piece of cardboard in the bottom of the bed, water it well, then empty a couple of growbags or compost bags into it.

above Recycled bricks make a quick raised bed ideal for children; line with cardboard to keep weeds down and retain moisture, then fill with compost before planting.
opposite Amelanchiers are the ideal tree for an average family garden, relatively compact in size and with beautiful blossom and autumn colour.

Five no-maintenance plants for a busy family

If you want plants that need hardly any attention, these are for you...

Japanese anemone (*Anemone x hybrida*)

Flowering from late summer to mid-autumn, this elegant plant sends up white or pink flowers almost a metre high. Plant it at the back of a border and watch it spread over the years. Just cut the dead flower stems down when they have finished.

Make more plants by: division, page 117.

Verbena bonariensis

Lofty, vivid-purple-topped wiry stems give any garden a look of naturalistic elegance and butterflies love the flowers. Tall enough to be impressive but transparent enough to be see-through – a winning combination. Plus, they need no staking.

Make more plants by: transplanting self-sown seedlings, page 112.

Snowy mespilus or June berry (*Amelanchier lamarckii*)

A perfect tree for a family garden, this has it all: a stunning white cloud of blossom in spring and coppery young leaves turning yellowish green and then red in the autumn. In high summer it has red berries and even in winter the bare branches make an attractive crown-like shape. No real pruning is necessary, but if you do want to give it a snip, do it in winter.

Big blue lilyturf (*Liriope muscari)*

This evergreen grass soon forms a lush, dark green carpet even in that problem area, dry shade, and has the bonus of lovely purple flower spikes in the autumn. Needs no maintenance other than the removal of dead leaves in spring. Keep costs down by buying one plant, letting it clump up and then, after a couple of years, divide it to make more. Or, if you know anyone with this plant see if you can dig up a bit of it.

Make more plants by: division, page 117.

Silver grass (*Miscanthus sinensis* 'Morning Light')

A particularly beautiful grass with an arching fountain of narrow silver and green striped leaves, which reaches almost 2m high. Simply cut dead foliage and old fowered stems to the ground in spring. Plant it in full sun.

Make more plants by: division, page 117.

You can sometimes find small snowy mespilus trees at discount stores. These are super cheap but will take several years to get to a decent size. Alternatively, shop around for the best deal online for a 10-litre pot specimen.

The prairie garden

A stylised mimicry of natural prairies or meadows dominated by grasses and other perennials, this type of garden lends itself wonderfully to rural, informal locations, but it can look really striking in an urban landscape too. The High Line Park in New York, designed by Piet Oudolf, may be its crowning achievement – a ribbon of wild meadow threading above the city traffic.

The prairie garden is ideal for lazy gardeners who like a naturalistic landscape. If you have a sunny open location and poor dry soil, this could be the style for you, since these plants prefer free-draining, relatively low-fertility soil. Maintenance is minimal since most plants are perennial, lasting for many years. Many require little more than a chop to the ground in early spring. It's also ideal for wildlife lovers because most of the perennials are high in nectar and attract lots of pollinating insects, and seed heads left on plants over winter to provide structure also provide plenty of food for birds.

Sharp lines don't fit with a prairie garden, so hard landscaping tends to be minimal, with gravel being the material of choice for paths that bend and meander. Plants, though, can be on the expensive side, since most are perennials that are bought as plants rather than seeds. Mature grasses in particular can be surprisingly expensive, so how do you plant up a prairie garden on a budget?

How to plant a prairie garden: **style tips**

Although the intended effect of this sort of garden is to look natural, it must be planned quite carefully or it can end up looking like a mess. Aim to use a maximum of about 12 different plants within an average garden to maintain a sense of unity.

Plant each variety in groups of at least three plants to avoid a bitty look – they will soon meld together and look like one large plant. The only exception to this when using large specimen plants such as *Stipa gigantea* or *Melianthus Major*, which are impressive enough to stand alone. Once you've chosen your plants, repeat the groups throughout the garden in a loose pattern.

Avoid straight lines or neat block planting; plant in curvy drifts – teardrop shapes or wavy bands look natural and less contrived.

left The fluffy shaving brush leaves and flowerheads of Mexican feather grass wave in the wind.
right Repeat groups of the same plant throughout the garden to create a unified scheme.

Prairie garden planting

When you are starting a prairie garden from scratch, don't feel you have to fill every inch straight away; a garden can be a work in progress. Why not buy one or three (always avoid even numbers in naturalistic plantings) of each perennial or grass to start with? If you have a friend who has this style of garden you may even be able to avoid buying any plants at all – see How to Make New Plants for Free, page 108, for easy propagation techniques.

While you wait for the permanent plants to become established, fill the gaps with meadow-style annuals, sown directly into the space in spring. A few packets of seeds from the list below won't set you back much. The annuals will provide a wonderful, colourful, meadow-style background and avoid areas of bare earth. Repeat this technique for a year or two until your perennials are established enough to start propagating from. This way you will build up a whole garden of perennials for little cost.

Naturalistic meadow annuals to sow in gaps

Bishop's flower (*Ammi majus*)
Cornflower (*Centaurea cyanus*)
Californian poppy (*Eschscholzia californica*)
Field poppy (*Papaver rhoeas*)
White laceflower (*Orlaya grandiflora*)
Corncockle (*Agrostemma githago*)

Get the look: 10 prairie garden must-haves

Mexican feather grass (*Stipa tenuissima*)
This fluffy shaving brush of a grass is great planted in groups of at least three. Its fine stems wave in the slightest breeze and its toasted bronze colour gives gardens an exotic, dry feel.
Make more plants by: transplanting self-sown seedlings, page 112.

Golden oats (*Stipa gigantea*)
This is a magnificent impact plant; a dense clump of green grass topped by delicate 2m-high flowering stems that just seem to float. Plant it in the centre of a bed where you can see through the airy golden flower heads.
Make more plants by: division, page 117.

Feather reed-grass (*Calamagrostis x acutiflora* 'Karl Foerster')
This narrow, upright grass makes a good contrast with looser, wavier prairie-style plants. The toasted-brown flowering stems look particularly great in winter. Plant in groups of three or more for the best effect. Established clumps can be divided after three years.
Make more plants by: division, page 117.

Plume thistle (*Cirsium rivulare* 'Atropurpureum')
Reaching more than a metre high, this glamorous plant has gorgeous deep crimson thistles dancing on top of deep green serrated foliage.
Make more plants by: division, page 117.

Globe thistle (*Echinops ritro* 'Veitch's Blue')
From mid- to late summer these spiky blue flower balls punctuate the border, standing more than a metre high. This plant has a stiff, architectural quality that makes a nice contrast with wavy grasses.
Make more plants by: taking root cuttings/division, page 114/117.

Mullein (*Verbascum bombyciferum*)
This silvery, felty-leaved plant sends up towering flower spikes more than 2m high. Even when the bright yellow flowers fade the stems are impressive, like gargantuan candelabras. It's a biennial, meaning it simply grows in the first year then flowers and dies in the second. Luckily it self-sows all over the place, so if you buy just one plant over two consecutive years you will have flowering plants forever.
Make more plants by: transplanting self-sown seedlings, page 112.

left *Ammi majus* creates delightful cow parsley-like clouds of flowers that help to knit other plants together.
above Tall *Verbascum bomficyferum* makes a focal point in a sunny bed.

Miss Wilmott's ghost (*Eryngium giganteum*)
A spectral skeleton of silver stems, serrated leaves and an extraordinary spiky flower make this more armour than plant. Give it sun and a dry spot and it will thrive.
Make more plants by: taking root cuttings, page 114.

Ice plant (*Sedum spectabile*)
This fleshy-leaved glaucous plant quickly makes a dense clump, making this a good anchor for airier plants. The pink flowers from late summer are beloved by butterflies and it provides useful shape and form over winter.
Make more plants by: division, page 117.

above The vivid pink flowers of *Sedum spectabile* are welcome in autumn and seedheads provide good form over winter.
right Lofty flowering stems of *Stipa gigantea* or golden oats.

Salvia nemorosa 'Caradonna'
Purple flower spikes form a profusion of neat exclamation marks atop a dense green cushion of leaves that smell of sage. Best planted en masse, such as in a ribbon throughout a border, but each plant takes up only about 30cm so planting in this way can be expensive. Start with a few plants and divide or take cuttings from them when they become established.
Make more plants by: taking stem cuttings/division, page 116/117.

Donkey-tail spurge (*Euphorbia myrsinites*)
More like dinosaur tails than its name would imply, this drought-loving plant looks great planted in groups of three at the edge of a border where it can spill out. The flowers are low and less showy than the extraordinary spiky leaves, made up of what look like interlocking triangles.
Make more plants by: transplanting self-sown seedlings, page 112.

How to lay a gravel path

Meandering gravel paths are a classic feature of prairie gardens and it's not too difficult to lay your own. Mark out the path with line paint, then dig down by 10cm, adding the soil you have dug out to the beds. If you don't mind gravel escaping into your beds, no edging is necessary, but if you want a cleaner finish, flexible mild steel edging is easy to install and, though not inexpensive, may be worth the investment. Bash down the soil along the path with the head of a rake so it is compacted. If the soil is still soft, add a layer of hardcore (crushed brick or stone) and if deep-rooted weeds are a problem, add weed suppressing membrane to stop them coming through. Then rake over your gravel to completely cover.

Savvy Tip

Many ornamental grasses, such as golden oats and feather reed-grass retain their toasted golden flower heads over winter. Simply remove old flower heads and brown foliage in early spring to allow new growth to emerge. Leaving the stems to stand in the coldest months not only creates some interesting shapes, especially when frosted or backlit by low winter sun, but also provides food for seed-eating birds.

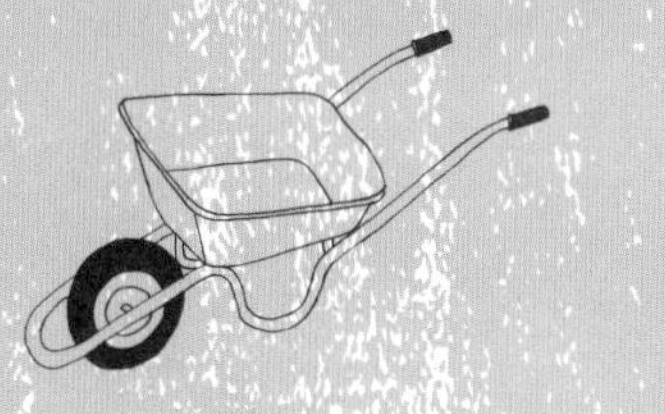

Grow Food for Peanuts

Growing food is arguably the very best kind of gardening – it's fantastically rewarding and the fruits of your labour are delicious. But growing your own doesn't automatically mean you will save money. It's easy to rack up quite a bill on fruit bushes and vegetable plants and seeds, not to mention the raised beds, compost and feeds that seem to go with it. Certain fruits and vegetables are so cheap to buy that going to all the bother of growing them can seem a false economy, especially when, at the end of it all, you only have a couple of tiny aubergines and one green pepper to show for your pains.

But growing food really is worth it. As long as you grow the right crops and follow a few simple rules you'll end up with organic produce that you'd pay a premium for in the shops, and picked so fresh it will be sweeter, crunchier, riper and more flavourful than anything you can buy. That really does sound worth the hassle.

Three ways to save money when growing your own fruit and vegetables

1. Choose crops that are worth growing

Lettuce? Yes. Aubergines? Don't waste your time. See Crops Worth Growing (page 88–97) for more information.

2. Share an 'instant garden' delivery

If sowing seed seems too much hassle or you just don't have the space to do it, don't rule out the idea of an 'instant' vegetable garden, bought online. These can be surprisingly good value if you choose a large delivery and split the plug plants with a friend.

3. Don't waste money on expensive kit

You really don't need metal wigwams, arches or other hullaballoo. Make your own with willow, hazel or bamboo canes. Many fruit and vegetables grow very well in pots but you don't have to stump up for expensive ones – containers can be upcycled or simply cheap and cheerful. As for raised beds, do you really need them at all?

Before you begin: raised bed or on the level?

Recently, it has become an accepted fact that to grow food you need a raised bed. People everywhere are spending their weekends sawing boards and bashing in stakes. But they might not need to. Raised beds are only really necessary if you have particularly heavy soil that doesn't let water drain away, resulting in soggy roots and unhappy plants. You can work out if you need a raised bed with a simple test. Dig a hole about 30cm in diameter and 30cm deep and fill it with a bucket of water. Once this has drained, fill it again. If this has disappeared within 24 hours, the drainage in your soil is good enough to grow plants in directly. If any water is still there, a raised bed would be better for you. See How Not to Waste Your Money on Gardening Kit, page 132, for ideas on how to make them.

Savvy Tip

Don't be berry snobby: Pound stores, cut-price supermarkets or 99p shops are a treasure trove for fruit bushes. You can buy raspberries, blackcurrants, grapevines, gooseberries and all manner of fruit bushes in the aisles for the price of a bottle of water. Just be careful to choose only the healthiest specimens, since life under strip lighting is not ideal. Ask a shop worker when they are getting in a new delivery and time your return to snap up some healthy bargains.

Crops worth growing

When you're growing food on a budget, the crops you choose are really important. These 30 crops are fun to grow, look great in your garden and won't waste your time or money. Sow them in newspaper pots for a free start (see page 122) and why not save your seed so you won't have to buy new seed next year (see page 110)?

10 'just a little bit' crops

These are the ones that you find quietly rotting in the bottom of your fridge three weeks later. We've all discovered a mushy plastic bag of herbs, salad or what was once a cucumber. It's because you eat a little bit of these crops at a time, so buying a whole packet doesn't make sense. Grow them yourself and you can pick a bit here and there, graze, or harvest crops small so you won't waste anything.

1. Herbs

This is a massive group of plants, from large woody perennials such as rosemary and sage to delicate annuals like Thai basil. Thyme, tarragon, chives, parsley, oregano, mint... the list is long and all are worth growing if you like eating them. Most herbs are beautiful, free-flowering plants that bring in pollinators, so they are worth including in any garden and are also really easy to propagate so you may well not have to buy them at all. Many herbs are perennials so will need little effort once you've got them established – and since you'll only need a leaf or sprig here and there, they will definitely save you money in the long term. Never again will you have to scratch your head when faced with a recipe requiring a tablespoon of chopped sage and have to dash out to the supermarket. Use them fresh, then really get the most out of them when the season is over by preserving gluts, whether you're drying lemon verbena for mid-winter tisanes or making jars of mint and apple jelly.

2. Chillies

One chilli plant can produce up to 50 fruits and a recipe rarely calls for the use of more than two. Grow them, and you can pick them and eat them fresh over the growing season, wincing over the different scales of heat as they turn from green to fiery red. On top of that, you'll get to choose from a dizzying list of varieties, from Jalapeño to Thai bird's eye and other kinds you won't be able to buy in the shops. Sow in mid-spring inside and transplant outside to larger pots (up to 30cm diameter) in early summer.

3. Garlic

Growing your own garlic really does make financial sense. Each head of garlic contains about 10 bulbs, each of which will grow into a new head of garlic. So you'll get about 100 individual bulbs from one bought head of garlic. That is a lot of pasta sauce.

By far the most cost-effective way to grow garlic is from supermarket bulbs, since these are way cheaper than those from specialist suppliers and garden centres. However, you will take a bit of a chance since they may not be a variety suitable for our climate. Indeed, you probably won't know what variety they are at all. However, since the costs are so minimal, it's probably a risk worth taking and the worst that can happen is that you'll end up with smaller bulbs.

Plant garlic in autumn, placing each individual clove just below the soil surface about 20cm apart (pointy end up) and harvest the following summer when the lower leaves turn brown, carefully digging them up and leaving them to dry in a well-ventilated place for three weeks. When the skins and leaves turn papery you can roughly plait the leaves of the bulbs together and hang them up. You can then use the garlic throughout autumn and into winter.

4. Cucumbers

A homegrown cucumber, eaten small, is a marvellous thing, crunchy, sweet and refreshing with none of the watery sliminess of supermarket cucumbers. Surprisingly productive, cucumbers thrive in containers and grow bags as well as in open ground with plenty of organic matter added. You should get about 10 cucumbers per plant.

5. Sorrel

It's difficult to get hold of this delicious lemony-sharp salad leaf in the shops. As if this wasn't reason enough to grow it, it's also a perennial, meaning once bought you won't have to buy it again and it is there in early spring, just when there is nothing else to harvest. It's perfect for soups, in omelettes or added into sauces for fish. The perennial variety is known as broad-leaved sorrel; the more delicate annual variety is called buckler's leaf sorrel and is better for salads that you grow from seed. If you know anyone growing broad-leaved sorrel, why not ask if you could dig up a piece to replant at home?

6. Lamb's lettuce

Sometimes called corn salad or mache, this, along with rocket, watercress and lettuce, is what makes up many of our much-loved (and much thrown away) supermarket salad bags. Its mild flavour makes it a good foil for the pepperiness of some other leaves and it will grow all through the winter. It's very slow growing, but if you wait for each plant to mature before harvesting, a row of plants will go a very long way.

7. Salad rocket

Unlike its perennial cousin wild rocket, this invaluable peppery salad leaf will only last a few months before bolting, but it is so productive that it's well worth growing, especially when buying organic bags of the stuff can be so pricey. Sow it outside where you want to grow it – in a large pot, window box or vegetable bed – in autumn or early spring and watch out for flea beetle. Re-sow every three weeks for a constant supply, pulling up plants when they start to flower.

8. Lettuce

More than half of all the bagged salad we buy from supermarkets goes to waste. Grow it yourself and you'll not only save money but cut down on what you throw away. You can grow it all year round; seed is cheap, there are countless varieties from frilly to cos, purple to green and all are a cinch to grow. All you need is some soil or compost. Lettuce will thrive in a window box or pot and do just as well in the ground. It isn't too fussy about sun – in fact it prefers partial shade – and you won't need to feed it either. Keep an eye out for slugs and snails.

It's easy to save lettuce seed. Leave a few plants to set seed, avoiding any that bolt or set seed early, since you don't want this characteristic to be passed down to your next generation. A couple of weeks after the lettuce plant has flowered, shake the seeds into a paper bag. Repeat this every day until all the seeds have been collected. Then dry and store them as normal.

Cucumber plants can be susceptible to rotting at the base if they get too cold and wet. Planting them inside a 'collar' made from a plastic bottle, and watering only outside this collar, helps keep the stem dry.

9. Watercress

This refreshing peppery leaf is perfect for adding to salads to pep them up. You rarely want more than few sprigs at a time so it makes more sense to grow it yourself than buy a whole bag of the stuff. All you need to do is sow seeds into a large pot of compost placed either in a saucer of water or on a piece of fabric (an old woollen jumper should do) to keep the compost moist.

10. Potatoes

Big potatoes – those workhorses of the kitchen that we mash, boil, chip and roast – are not expensive to buy, let's be honest. But it's never fun to throw vegetables away. And, unless you are super organised and/or cook for a family of 16, chances are you won't get through a plastic bag of supermarket spuds without them turning green and sprouting in all directions. Shop-bought potatoes don't last that long because they have been washed before bagging. Unwashed spuds, on the other hand, can last much longer because the skins are dry. If you grow and store your own potatoes, you won't have to throw any away.

To grow a decent supply of potatoes choose any maincrop variety and buy tubers in late winter or early spring. Lay these out in old egg boxes, so that the blunt end, where most of the eyes are, is uppermost. Place them on a windowsill inside to let shoots develop. Known as chitting, this process gives them a head start when you put them in the ground. If you are growing only in containers, give maincrops a miss and grow salad potatoes instead (see page 93).

In mid-spring, plant the chitted potatoes, sprouting ends up, about 30cm apart and 30cm deep in soil that has had plenty of organic matter added. As the plants grow, 'earth' them up by drawing soil around the base of the plants with a hoe or spade. This stops the potatoes turning green. Keep well watered throughout the summer and feed every couple of weeks.

Early autumn is the time to dig up your spuds. Two weeks before you harvest them, cut the plants down to ground level and compost them. This lets the skins of the potatoes harden up a bit so you don't damage them when lifting. Then, on a sunny, dry day, dig up carefully with a fork and leave to dry for a few hours before gently putting them in hessian or paper sacks and storing them in a frost-proof shed. Stored this way, the potatoes should keep for months.

right Maincrop potatoes such as Red Duke of York will last for months if stored properly.

Make a living salad wall

This is a fantastic way to harvest lots of salad crops from a tiny space. Plastic fruit crates can be got for free from a greengrocer, and crate-lining material can be bought cheaply from any garden centre. The latter is invaluable because it stops the compost falling out while still allowing water to get through.

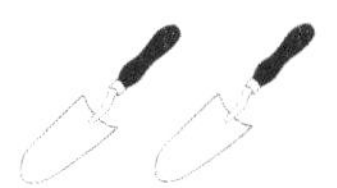

You will need

Weed-suppressing membrane
4 plastic fruit crates
Stapler with staples
Multipurpose, organic, peat-free compost
Perlite or sphagnum moss
Scissors
1 supermarket 'living salad' or lettuce seedlings
Cable ties
16 sticks narrow enough to poke through the holes in the crates; 8 cut slightly longer than the width of the crate, 8 slightly longer than the height.

When to do it

Spring to autumn

How to do it

First cut four pieces of weed-suppressing membrane that are big enough to line the sides and bottom of each crate and leave a flap at the bottom that can be folded up to form the front of the finished salad wall. Staple the membrane around the edges and to the bottom of the crate.

Fill your crates with a 50:50 mixture of compost and perlite or sphagnum moss. Make sure you fill each crate right up into the corners, since any gaps will cause the compost to drop down once you hang it vertically. Now fold up the flap of material to form the front, stapling this down to the edges too. Now make a grid at the front of the crate by poking sticks through the holes in the front of the crate; two sticks running across and two from top to bottom. This grid stops the compost from falling out.

You are now ready to plant. With your scissors, cut 14 equally spaced crosses in the membrane. Gently pull apart the root ball of your living salad to make several sections. Then, holding the largest leaves (not the stem or base) tease the plants apart so you have 14 single lettuce seedlings. Holding one seedling by its largest leaf, make a hole in the compost through one of the crosses with your other hand and drop the root ball into it, then cover with the compost and firm down. Repeat until all the holes are filled.

Place the planted-up crates flat on the ground out of direct sun and water well. Be sure to keep the compost moist over the next few days, since the plants will be very susceptible to drying out. Leave the crates flat on the ground for three or four days so the plants can settle in.

Attach the crates to horizontal railings or trellis by threading cable ties through holes in the back of the crates. Water from above; the water will trickle slowly down through the crates, irrigating all the plants along the way. Harvest as and when you want. Once a plant is finished, simply replace with another.

10 pricey-in-the-shops crops

If you want the freshest, best-tasting organic versions of these crops in the shops, you'll pay a premium for it. So why not grow your own luxury food aisle at home?

Why not do a tomato swap with friends so that everyone grows a different variety and you share out the plants?

1. Tomatoes – cherry or heirloom

Red, yellow, orange, purple, green and stripey, tomatoes grown at home can be all manner of exciting colours, shapes and sizes. You can get hold of some of these exotic-looking specimens in the supermarkets these days, but they'll cost you – especially if they're organic and 'on the vine'. So why not grow them yourself? That way, you can eat them when they're still warmed from the sun, not out of the chiller. Whether you go for yellow cherry 'Sungold', purple Black Krim, mini plum 'Santonio' or the classic sauce variety 'Costoluto Fiorentino', there's a variety to inspire.

Saving tomato seed is a little more complicated than many other seeds, but well worth it if you find a variety you particularly love. First, make sure it's not an F1 hybrid. Seeds from these varieties won't always 'come true' and can differ from the parent plant so you won't know what you're getting. Seed packets will clearly mark if a variety is an F1 hybrid or not. Cut a ripe tomato in half, scoop out the seeds and pulp and add them to the bottom of a glass. Fill the glass half-full with water, gently stir to combine, then set aside for three days.

After this, skim off any mould that has formed and mix again, topping up with a little more water. Three days later, any viable seed will have sunk to the bottom. Pour off the pulp and liquid and strain the seed into a sieve, then spread out to dry on a plate for several days before drying and storing as normal.

2. Raspberries

These velvety berries are a must for growing yourself since you can pick them when they are perfectly ripe. The very reason raspberries are so delectable – their softness – means that they don't keep for long. Shop-bought raspberries tend either to be sour and underripe or already turning mouldy in the punnets. And they're scarily expensive too. Grow them yourself and gorge in abandon. Then make jam from any that are left over.

3. Sweetcorn

Just-picked sweetcorn, thrown in boiling water or tossed on the barbecue, is one of the great gourmet pleasures. You get to eat it before any of those sugars have turned to starch, avoiding the clagginess of some bought sweetcorn and maximising its natural crunchy sweetness. Even if each plant only produces two or three cobs, it's worth it. Sweetcorn is best grown in the ground, but it will be surprisingly happy in a large container too.

4. Fancy salad potatoes

Miniature salad potatoes are all the rage in supermarkets these days, but they are just regular salad potatoes, dug up when they're still small. Try a small First Early such as 'Mimi' or 'Rocket' for super early mini potatoes by early summer. Jersey Royals can be yours too – buy 'International Kidney' tubers and dig them up after 12 weeks. And for a really flash salad potato, try 'Pink Fir Apple', a firm, knobbly, waxy spud that adds class to any salad. If this doesn't satisfy your potato adventurousness, you could try blue or purple potatoes. A French variety called 'Vitelotte' has a marvellously chestnutty taste and is dark blue all the way through. Small salad potatoes can easily be grown in containers, too, because you will be harvesting them while still small. Dig them up after about 8 weeks.

Savvy tip

You can get two crops of salad potatoes for the price of one if you hold back a few tubers in spring and put them in the fridge. In late summer once you have harvested your first crop, plant these 'cold-stored' tubers. By Christmas you should have some delicious new potatoes to go with your turkey.

left Organic heritage and cherry tomatoes on the vine go for a premium in supermarkets; grow them yourself and reap the benefits.
right Sweetcorn eaten soon after harvest is far superior to that bought in the shops and will grow surprisingly well in a large container.

5. Globe artichokes

Even a small garden should have a couple of these majestic, silver-leaved plants. The delicious artichokes they produce are almost a lucky bonus. You should get up to 12 artichokes per mature plant which, when picked and eaten fresh, are sweeter and more delectable than any you can buy.

6. Peaches

Much like apricots, these sweet fruits often lack flavour when you buy them in the shops, a victim of their short shelf life, because they have to be picked before they're fully ripe in order to get them to the shops before they rot. Grow them yourself and you can pick them when they're so ripe the juice will dribble down your T-shirt. A 'Saturn' peach tree is a particularly desirable thing, producing doughnut-shaped fruits with sweet white flesh. Grow as for apricots (see page 94).

7. Figs

A fig tree is a beautiful thing, with its large, aromatic leaves smelling like dusty Mediterranean hillsides. And they really will produce fruit, even in cooler climates. Go for 'Brown Turkey' if at all in doubt about your garden's microclimate, but if you know you can offer a protected, warm spot you could try 'Dauphine'. Eat them standing up right there next to the tree.

8. Blueberries

Home-grown blueberries tend to be firmer and tangier than shop-bought ones that have been flown in from hotter climes. You may not harvest punnets-full in a day, but as most of us eat only a handful of blueberries at a time, this is no drawback. Fluffy mouldy blueberries can be a thing of the past if you grow a couple of bushes – try 'Sunshine Blue' or 'Bluecrop' – in containers filled with ericaceous compost (they like an acid soil). Swirl out the remains of your coffee pot every morning into the pots to keep the soil acidic. Since each bush should last at least 10 years, they will more than pay for themselves.

9. Apricots

They can be woolly or hard as ping-pong balls when on offer in the shops, but when you grow apricots yourself, it's a whole different story. Perfectly ripe, aromatic, ambrosial apricots can be yours if you buy a tree and train it as a fan against a sunny sheltered wall or fence. Apricot trees produce blossom early in spring when pollinating insects are not yet in flight, so you might have to help with the pollination – a make-up brush dabbed into the flowers usually does the trick – but the rewards in a good summer are definitely worth it. You can buy ready-trained fan-shaped trees, but they do tend to be pricey. Instead, buy a one-year old tree and train it yourself, pruning out all branches that grow inwards or back towards the fence and tying others to diagonal canes tied to horizontal wires. Only prune in summer, though, because winter pruning can encourage fungal disease. Apricots can also be grown in a pot.

10. French beans

Regimented rows of beans in cellophane, flown in from many miles away, feature in pretty much everyone's supermarket trolley these days. We throw a lot of them away, and you'll pay extra if you want them to be organic. So why not cut down on your food miles by growing them at home? Happy in pots or open ground, you can either grow climbing varieties that will romp up a wigwam (yellow 'Golden Gate' are fun, while green 'Cobra' are wonderfully reliable) or there are dwarf varieties that won't need supporting, such as yellow 'Rocquencourt' or colourful 'Purple Teepee'. Who says beans have to be green?

Go go grow bags

A great source of good cheap compost for fruit and vegetables in containers is that in grow bags. Shops tend to discount grow bags from midsummer onwards after the main tomato planting season has ended, so this is a great time to snap up a few bargains. Either empty the compost into pots or simply cut the bags in half vertically so you end up with two decent bags you can stand upright. If you don't like the look of the plastic, pop each in a hessian sack or wrap a piece of bamboo screening around them.

10 mega producers

Some crops give a lot back; even a couple of plants of these accommodating fruit and vegetables will produce a harvest to fill your plate.

1. Summer squash

Huge plants but a massive harvest to match. As fast as you cut these courgette-like fruits, they will produce a new one. Delicious when picked small (no bigger than a peach) and steamed. Yellow patty pan squash 'Sunbeam' is particularly prolific and the long curly green squashes of 'Tromboncino', which will clamber up a fence, trellis or wigwam, are always a talking point. Watch for mildew, see page 154, and keep plants well fed. All that growing and producing takes it out of a plant.

2. Chard

Find me an allotment without chard and I'll give you a jar of chutney. But this spinach-like vegetable is popular for good reason. It's delicious steamed, has beautiful colourful stems (if you buy the Swiss chard variety 'Bright Lights') and one plant will produce enough leaves for a week of suppers. Chard will grow all year round (particularly the hardier 'White Silver') and is just as happy in pots as it is in the ground. One for any vegetable plot, however tiny, leaf miner is its only real enemy (see page 154).

3. Kale

When all else in the midwinter garden is gloomy, kale will give you hope. Nutritious, prolific and handsome, the crepe-like leaves of 'Cavolo Nero' or frilly plumes of 'Red Russian' seem to defy the winter cold – you can even pick it in the snow. Sow it in the summer and you'll have fresh leaves from autumn to spring when the flowering shoots will start to appear. Leave these and you'll get a bonus crop rather like the tenderest sprouting broccoli.

4. Courgette

Like summer squash, these sprawling beasts take up some space (though a large container will suit them fine). Why not try a yellow courgette such as 'Soleil' or round one like 'Eight Ball'? Stripey 'Romanesco' brings a gourmet touch. Just a trio of plants will keep you in courgettes over the summer – any more than that and you might have to get the chutney jars out!

5. Jerusalem artichokes

The tubers of Jerusalem artichokes form underground, where they can stay for months on end. This means you can just dig them up whenever you want them. No waste. The tall, sunflower-like plants make a useful windbreak and, once planted, you won't have to do it again since any tubers left underground will come up again next year. They make possibly the best soup known to mankind.

left Figs are particularly productive if fan-trained against a sunny wall, but will also be happy in a large pot as long as they are not allowed to dry out.
right Courgettes such as stripy 'Romanesco' will produce all summer if you keep picking them and ensure the plants are well fed and watered.

6. Plums and greengages

Forget those crunchy round bullets the supermarkets sell, the Victoria plum is the real deal. So ripe the skin is only just holding in the juice, a home-picked plum is the true taste of midsummer. Finding Victoria plums or greengages – just like plums, but green – in the shops is almost impossible. Buy a one-year-old tree and give it a sunny or partially shady spot and within a year or two you'll be stuffing your face. These trees will be happy in a pot too.

7. Runner beans

A wigwam can produce enough tender green ribbons to satisfy most bean fans, and the flowers are as pretty as anything in the ornamental garden. They're a cinch to grow, needing nothing but water (lots of it) and feeding every fortnight. The large seeds are easy to sow direct – just watch out for slugs and snails. 'Scarlet Emperor' can't be beaten. Pick them young or they can be offputtingly stringy. If the seeds have started to swell and pods bend rather than snap, they're already too old. Ensure you don't leave mature beans on the plant, since this signals the plant to stop producing new flowers.

8. Kai-lan

Tasting like a cross between pak choi and broccoli, this oriental vegetable is a jack-of-all-trades. You can eat the shoots, the leaves and even the flowers, making it perfect for stir-fries or simply steamed. Best of all, even though the plant will die down over winter it should perk up the following spring, so once you've sown kai-lan once you should have it for several years.

9. Wild rocket

The perennial cousin of the slightly less peppery salad rocket, this deserves a place in any veg garden. It will grow in a pot or the ground and churn out delicious spicy leaves for several years, even well into the coldest winters. Watch out for flea beetle, see page 155.

10. Nasturtiums

Known for its profusion of cheery flowers, this sprawling plant makes a great summer screen for an ugly wall or fence – especially if you buy a trailing variety – but is also a great cropper, see right. Once you've grown nasturtiums once, they'll come back year after year.

Savvy tip

Not only can you eat the beautiful, delicate flowers of nasturtiums in salads (they are deliciously peppery), but the leaves can be chopped and eaten fresh and the seed pods pickled. Simply soak them in brine for 24 hours then drain, pour them into a jar, add tarragon or a couple of bay leaves and cover them with vinegar.

Planting a vegetable garden

Location

A sunny, open site sheltered from wind is the ideal spot. Avoid anywhere overhung by mature trees or in full shade, but partial shade (anywhere that gets at least four hours of direct sun a day) will be all right if you have no other option. Remember your vegetable crops will need regular watering so try not to site them too far from a water source.

How to make a vegetable bed

Once you have decided on a location, mark out your vegetable beds. Obviously you want to maximise the growing area, but access to the crops is key too. You don't want to make the beds so wide that you can't reach the crops easily. A good way to work out the ideal width is to squat down and reach forward as though you were picking something – don't overstretch, it should be comfortable. This should be the mid point of your bed. The length of the bed is less important, though you don't want it to be so long that walking round it is awkward.

To make the bed, use a garden spade to edge the perimeter and then dig over the area with a fork. If you are turning an area of grass into a vegetable bed, remove the turf first (see page 56). If making a raised bed simply turn the turf upside down and bury it in the lower level of the bed. Dig down to a fork's depth, then bash the soil up with the back of the fork to break down any clumps. Remove large stones and weeds as you go. Any perennial weeds such as dock, brambles or nettles will only multiply if you add them straight to your compost bin so put them in a bin bag first until they rot down, or make them into liquid plant food (see page 145). If the area is too large to contemplate digging over by hand, another technique is to lay black plastic over the area, weighed down with stones. Leave this for at least six months and any weeds will die. The soil can then be dug more easily. Yet another way to clear ground is to spray it with glyphosate, which will kill any growth over a period of about three weeks. But for a regular-sized vegetable bed, hand digging is the way to go.

Perfect paths

Make sure you leave a path wide enough to push a wheelbarrow between any of your vegetable beds. If you leave the paths as grass, you will have to mow them regularly. If you have raised beds, the mower won't get right up to the edges so you'll have to get out the garden shears too. Save yourself hassle by laying weed-suppressing membrane or mulch mat on your paths (affordable and available from all garden centres). You can sprinkle bark chippings on top to make it look more natural. Alternatively, leave the paths as grass but go for regular, flat beds so you can easily mow right up to the edges. A metal edging that can be pushed into the ground flush with the grass will stop grass encroaching on the beds and make it easy to keep the edges neat. Buying galvanised metal edging by the roll is not expensive and will save you hours of weeding and edging in the long run.

Raised or on the level?

Unless you are gardening on a solid surface such as a terrace, or your soil is particularly heavy (see below) or poor draining, raised beds won't grow any better vegetables than regular beds. They do keep things tidy, though, and can deter weeds from encroaching on your vegetables. If you do decide to go for raised beds you can either make your own (see page 131) or buy a kit – there are some very affordable ones available. But bear in mind you will still have to put the kit together, dig over the soil base and find some topsoil to fill the bed with.

Prepare the soil

Vegetables take a lot of fertility out of the soil when they grow, so you need to put a lot in. Some soils are naturally fertile, but all benefit from the addition of well-rotted organic matter in the shape of garden compost, well-rotted farmyard manure or spent mushroom compost. This adds nutrients and 'heft' to the soil and improves drainage. So if you haven't already got a compost bin on the go, start one now (see page 139). Work out what sort of soil you have by doing the handful test on page 9, then add organic matter. To clay, chalky and sandy soils aim for a layer at least 10cm thick, for loam you can get away with 5cm. Every time you harvest a crop, add some more organic matter.

What crop where?

To get the best harvest from your crops and minimise disease it's a good idea to practise crop rotation. Crops basically split into four groups – legumes, roots and onions, brassicas and potato - and each group has its own demands on the soil.

Legumes - peas, beans
Roots and onions – carrots, beetroot, garlic, leeks, parsnips, shallots
Brassicas – cabbages, broccoli, kale
Potato – potatoes, tomatoes, aubergines, peppers

It is not a good idea to grow the same group in the same patch of soil year after year since diseases can build up and the soil can become depleted of nutrients. So we tend to rotate the groups over a four-year cycle which manages the nutrients in the soil the most effectively.

Year 1 – legumes
Year 2 – roots and onions
Year 3 – brassicas
Year 4 – potatoes

Perennial crops such as asparagus and herbs can be grown elsewhere and salads, courgettes, squashes or cucumbers can be slotted in wherever you like.

If you only have room for one bed, follow the same principle, rotating crops around each area of soil within the bed over a four-year cycle.

3 steps to success

Now you are ready to get growing. There are three secrets to success with growing vegetables, particularly if space is limited.

1. Only grow crops worth the effort (see Grow Food for Peanuts, page 84, for ideas).

2. Check on your vegetable garden little and often. It's only then that you'll notice the weeds, the plants that need tieing in, the beginnings of mildew. You'll also know when the strawberries will be at the peak of ripeness. If you spot things early you can get onto them straight away and they will be much easier to sort out. A quick, regular sweep over with a hoe will despatch weeds before they turn into triffids. A daily 5-minute visit to your veg garden will ultimately save you hours.

3. Think ahead. As one crop matures in the bed, have another in the wings, ready to plant out when there is a gap. Sowing into small pots either on a windowsill (from early spring) or outside (from spring to autumn) means you will always have crops coming on. It is easy to fill your beds from spring to summer, but don't forget there are plenty of crops to grow over winter too.

5 indispensable crops to grow over summer

Tomatoes
French beans
Potatoes
Carrots
Peas

5 indispensable crops to grow over winter

Garlic
Shallots
Onions
Leeks
Winter salads

One pot, ten crops: How to grow food in one container all year round

Many of us don't have the space to grow food in the ground, so we rely on containers instead. Pots can be surprisingly productive but we don't always maximise their potential. With just one relatively large pot, you could harvest 10 different crops in a single year if you combine compatible plants and plan the growing year carefully. The crops here are divided into three growing seasons. So even if you only have a tiny balcony, you could be harvesting a plethora of fresh, home-grown vegetables all year round.

You will need

1 large pot – a rubber tub trug is ideal or any plastic pot at least 45cm diameter (see Give cheap plastic pots the sack, page 45, for a way to make them more attractive)

Household drill and drill bit if no drainage holes

Multipurpose, organic, peat-free compost

A wigwam support made from bamboo canes or any strong flexible sticks such as willow (see How to make a willow wigwam, page 128)

How to do it

Drill several drainage holes in the base of the container if necessary, fill with compost and push in the wigwam support. Now plant up according to the time of year.

right Cherry tomatoes, green and purple lettuce and cucumbers share a pot in mid summer.

Late spring to early summer

You will need

3 tomato plants (a cordon or staking variety such as 'Sungold' or 'Gardener's Delight')
2 cucumber plants such as 'Ridge Perfection' or 'Rocky'
Up to 8 lettuce plants

How to do it

Plant the tomatoes and cucumbers next to a vertical support, evenly spaced apart, and tie in. Fill the gaps with lettuce plants. Water well. Once fruits have set on the tomatoes and cucumber, feed fortnightly (see page 145). Place in a sunny, sheltered position and tie the climbing plants into the supports as they grow. Watch out for mildew on the cucumber leaves (see page 154) and pinch out sideshoots on the tomatoes regularly to encourage plants to produce more fruit. By late summer, all of these crops will be over and can be removed to make space for the next ones.

Late summer to early autumn

You will need

3 kale plants such as 'Cavolo Nero' or 'Red Russian' (you can sow this in advance yourself in small pots in midsummer or buy plug plants)
4 chard plants such as 'Bright Lights' (raise as for kale, above)
Broad bean seeds for autumn sowing, such as 'Aquadulce Claudia'
5 early maturing garlic cloves such as 'Early Purple Wight'

How to do it

Remove your summer crops (see above) and the top 5cm of compost. Top up the pot with fresh compost and sow two broad bean seeds at the base of each vertical support, then plant the kale in the centre of the pot with the chard around the outside. Plant the garlic cloves by pushing them into the compost, pointy end up, so their tips are about 1cm under the surface. Water well.

The chard and kale can be cropped over autumn and winter but the biggest crops will come in spring. At this time, the broad beans will also set pods. Pinch out the growing tips of the broad bean plants (about the top 5cm) in spring – these are delicious steamed, and removing them will deter blackfly too.

Early to mid-spring

You will need

Salad rocket seed
Spring onion seed
Radish seed

How to do it

By mid-spring you should have harvested all your kale and chard, so there should be a few gaps in which to sow some radish, salad rocket and spring onion seeds. Simply sow a few on top of the compost and ruffle the surface slightly to cover them. Since these are quick-growing crops they will be ready to harvest within two months, leaving space for your summer crops.

By late spring, the early maturing garlic should be ready to harvest. You can eat this sort of garlic – known as green or softneck – straight away, with no need to dry and hang them. Leave the broad beans to mature – they will probably be ready by midsummer.

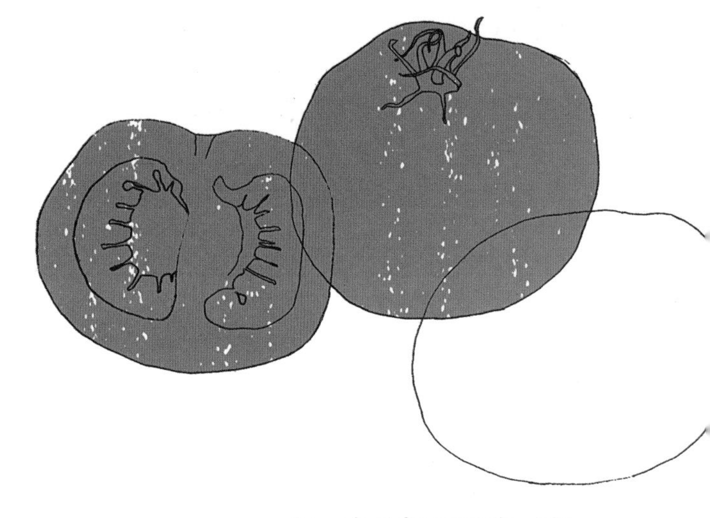

Planting a herb garden

Location

Most herbs like a sunny, open spot, so aim for this if at all possible. They also tend to like free-draining soil, so avoid areas that are soggy or compacted. Unless your soil is naturally light and free-draining (see page 87 for how to determine this), your herbs will probably be happiest in pots or raised beds. See page 131 for how to make a raised bed.

Herb garden design

If you have the space for it, an arrangement of four square raised beds around $1m^2$ and at least 20cm high divided by two paths crossing in the middle makes for a beautiful and easily accessible herb garden. Make sure the paths are wide enough to kneel down in so you can pick the herbs easily. Depending on the existing surface, paths can be gravel, grass, brick, stone or bark chips.

Prepare the soil

Once you have constructed your raised beds, dig over the existing soil to a garden fork's depth (if the area is lawn, see page 56 for how to remove the turf), then add topsoil or John Innes nos 2 or 3 so that the beds are about two-thirds full. Now add a third horticultural grit or perlite (volcanic rock fragments) to the soil to top them up (the levels will sink slightly as the soil settles) and mix it all together well. Adding the grit/perlite will ensure the roots of the herbs don't sit in water.

What herbs?

Simple really; grow what you like to eat. Like all plants, herbs can be perennial (live for several years), biennial (live for two years, flowering in the second one) or annual (lasting only one year). Perennial and biennial herbs can grow quite large while some annuals take up little space.

Even within the perennial group, there are distinctions, with some herbs disappearing below ground over winter and some remaining pretty much the same all year round. When you choose where to position your herbs, bear this in mind if you want to avoid large areas of bare soil during winter. Some perennials – such as mint – could be described as thugs as they are so invasive. They must be planted in a pot or they will take over everything else.

Buy or borrow?

Herb seeds and plants are not expensive to buy. To keep costs down, grow annual herbs from seed and buy relatively small specimens of perennial herbs that will soon catch up with larger potted versions. If you have friends with herb plants, you can also propagate free plants easily, whether by saving seed, dividing existing plants or taking cuttings. See How to Make Plants for Free, page 108, for ideas.

Thugs

Invasive herbs, such as mint and lemon balm, are best planted in a pot. If you want them within your herb bed, cut the bottom off the pot and sink it into the soil leaving 1cm of the rim sticking above the surface.

Designing with herbs

There's no reason why a herb garden can't be just as beautiful as a flower one. Think about structure, making sure each bed contains plants that will retain their form all year. A central focal point of upright rosemary, lavender or bay can hold a herb bed together. Think about edging too – chives or compact thyme varieties can make neat edgings while oregano or creeping thymes will trail down over the edges of the beds.

Foliage colours can be dramatic. Bring in purple with sage, basil, shiso or fennel; silver with thyme, rosemary, curry plant or common sage; yellow with thymes and golden oregano, and fresh green with parsley or coriander. Remember many herbs have beautiful flowers, from the blue of rosemary to white fluff of oregano and thyme, and purple pom poms of chives. Orange flowered marigolds will brighten up any herb bed and their flowers can be eaten in salad. Don't forget to consider shapes too. Feathery fennel or angelica makes a striking statement, reaching up to 2m high. Most herbs grow well together, but avoid planting fennel and dill next to each other since they will cross-pollinate, becoming 'fendill'. Avoid, too, planting different varieties of mint too close together since they tend to lose their individual scent and flavour.

You may want to sketch out a rough planting plan on paper before you start. Bear in mind the eventual size of the plants rather than the size they are when you buy them.

Perennial herbs that look good all year

– best grown from plants or cuttings

Rosemary
Lavender
Thyme
Winter savoury
Sage
Bay
Oregano/marjoram
Lemon verbena (needs protection over winter)
Fennel (dried stems can be left for winter structure)
Curry plant

Perennial herbs that disappear in winter

– best grown from plants/cuttings/division/seed

Mint
Tarragon (needs protection over winter)
Chives
Sorrel

Biennial herbs

– sow these every year

Parsley
Angelica

Annual herbs

– sow these in spring every year either in small pots or modules inside (from Feb-end-March) or directly into the soil outside (end-March-May)

Basil
Coriander (sow every couple of weeks for a constant supply)
Chervil
Dill
Shiso or perilla

Dare to be different

The best thing about growing your own herbs is that you can cook with unusual flavours and leaves that you can't buy in the shops. So to your regular Sweet Genovese basil, why not add aniseedy Thai basil? To garden mint add chocolate mint, lime mint or black peppermint. If you like rosemary and thyme, why not try winter savoury too? Throw a few lemon verbena leaves into boiling water for a zingy digestif, or grow shiso and make purple martinis.

Planting and aftercare

Before planting, set your plants out, still in their pots, on the surface of the soil. This helps get the positions right. Make a hole slightly larger than the pot, take out the plant and ruffle up the roots a little with your fingers to help them get going, then plant it at the same depth it was in the pot. Water at the initial planting but thereafter only when the soil is particularly dry. Trim back woody perennial herbs such as thyme, lavender and oregano after flowering to keep them neat, and harvest herbs regularly to keep them producing new leaves.

Harvesting herbs

When cutting herbs, aim to cut back to a growing point so that the plant can re-sprout, but never cut into the old (brown) wood since this can damage the plant. Regular harvesting keeps the plants bushy, discourages rot and also encourages more shoots to grow. The exceptions are coriander and chives which are cut to the ground. Chives will re-sprout while coriander must be re-sown regularly for a constant supply. Herbs have their strongest flavour just before they flower, so if you want to pick them for drying, aim to do it then. Always use scissors or secateurs to avoid bruising the stems.

Make five plants from one supermarket basil

We've all bought a lush-looking supermarket basil, popped it on the kitchen windowsill then looked on in dismay as, a week or so later, the plant dies. The reason is that supermarket herbs are actually many plants all squashed together in one pot. This makes them look lovely and healthy in the shop but means they run out of food and space after a couple of weeks so they flop over and die. Because the plants are so tightly packed, each one tries to grow up to the light, meaning leggy plants without many side shoots. All of this means that they will droop sooner or later and give up the ghost, unless, of course, you cut them back and divide them to give them the space, light and food they need to thrive.

Growing basil from seed can be slow and fiddly. One supermarket-bought herb will cost you less than a packet of seeds and you can end up with five healthy plants in minutes. You can divide plants all year round so you will always have fresh basil on your windowsill.

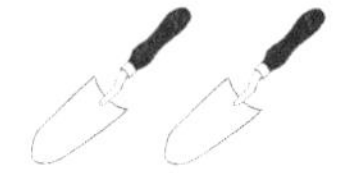

You will need

5 small plastic pots (about 9cm diameter)
Multipurpose, organic, peat-free compost
1 basil plant from a supermarket
Secateurs, scissors or a sharp knife

When to do it

All year round

Supermarket chives are even easier to split into new plants. Simply divide the root ball, as with basil, and plant each section about 20cm apart in garden soil.

How to do it

Fill your small plastic pots with compost. Take the bought basil plant and cut off any leggy shoots back to a strong pair of growing buds. You can eat the basil you chopped off.

Next, take the basil plant out of the pot and gently, without touching the stems or leaves of the plant, divide the rootball into five more or less equal-sized pieces. Each will probably have about three or four plants in it. Plant each section into a pot, pressing down gently and adding more compost so the plant is at the same level it was in the original pot.

Basil is susceptible to rotting if the leaves and stems are damp, so it is best to water young plants – particularly those with vulnerable cut stems such as these – from below. Place the pot in a lid, tray or other container and fill with a few centimetres of water. In time the shorn plants will recover and send out new growing shoots you can harvest. Once roots start to come out of the bottom of the pot, replant them into slightly larger pots.

Unless you are doing this in the height of summer, these plants will be happiest kept inside on a sunny windowsill.

Planting a fruit garden

Growing your own fruit is arguably even more rewarding than vegetables. Many fruit crops last for years, so after the initial planting there is little effort. Add to this the beautiful blossom, the shapes of the trees and bushes and the chance to pick fruit at its perfect point of ripeness, and it's a wonder more of us don't have a dedicated fruit garden.

Location

See Planting a Vegetable Garden, page 98. Most fruit needs plenty of sun to ripen well, though there are some shade tolerant crops such as redcurrants, cooking apples, acid cherries and blackberries. The perfect fruit garden would contain a warm south-facing wall.

Prepare the soil

See Planting a Vegetable Garden, page 98.

Designing a fruit garden

Fruit gardens lend themselves to a certain formality, where the shapes of the trees and bushes can be most appreciated and the fruit harvested easily. If you have space, an arrangement of three beds (two square and one rectangular) is ideal, along with two long borders for fruit trees – one against a wall (south or west facing if possible). Leave room on the paths for pots in which to grow blueberries and citrus fruits.

Suggested planting scheme for the ideal fruit garden

Square bed 1: Strawberries

Square bed 2: Rhubarb

Long rectangular bed: Raspberries (see right for how to make a support for raspberries)

Wall border: Espalier redcurrant bushes, fan-trained apricot and fig trees against the wall, underplanted with gooseberries and blackcurrant bushes.

Border screening fruit garden from rest of garden: Espalier apples and pear trees (check with suppliers that their pollination groups are compatible)

Pots: Blueberries, citrus trees (bring inside over winter)

Growing fruit against a wall or fence

If you have a wall or fence, this is the perfect place to grow fruit, particularly if it faces south or west. Not only will berry fruits grow happily against a wall, tied into horizontal wires, but fruit trees can be trained to grow flat against a wall, taking advantage of the heat soaked up by the bricks during the day. Peaches, cherries, figs, plums and apricots can be trained as fans, while apples and pears lend themselves to training as espaliers. Trained trees are not only beautiful to look at but highly productive for small spaces.

For ready-trained trees, go to a specialist fruit nursery and expect to pay more than for a standard (regular-shaped) tree. Alternatively, buy a maiden (one-year-old tree) and prune it yourself over several years to the required shape. There are plenty of guides online showing you how to do it, such as the RHS (see rhs.org.uk for more information).

Growing raspberries

While autumn-fruiting raspberries don't need any supports, summer-fruiting varieties do, and it is well worth doing this properly. Bash a couple of tree stakes into the ground at either end of the row and string galvanised metal wire tight between them. Screw hooks come in handy here since you can simply screw them into the wooden stakes and wrap the wire around the hook. Aim for three or four parallel horizontal wires. If the stakes threaten to fall inward due to the tension of the wires, a brick braced against the base of the stake underground usually does the trick.

Protecting your fruit

Of course, you're not the only one wanting to eat the fruits of your labours. Birds and other animals want them too. This is why most dedicated fruit gardens contain fruit cages, metal frames strung with string net to keep the pests off. These are not inexpensive, but will last a long time. Some fruit gardens are designed entirely within large fruit cages. If you can't stretch to a fruit cage, string old CDs or DVDs up among your fruit to deter birds, or buy smaller sections of netting to sling over beds once the fruit is ripening. Individual peaches or apricots can be protected with old stockings.

Buying fruit trees and bushes

Specialist fruit nurseries – look online – are fantastic resources and usually pretty good value. Cut-price supermarkets are also surprisingly good places to buy fruit bushes. But before you buy, check that you can't get plants for free. The following are all easy to grow from divisions or cuttings.

Beg before you buy: fruit for free

If you know someone who grows fruit and veg, ask if they could help you out with any of these and you won't have to spend a thing...

Rhubarb
a clump can be divided to make a new plant.

Blackcurrants
cut stems to ground level in winter and pot up till rooted to make new bushes.

Strawberries
peg down runners to make new plants, see page 115.

Raspberries
dig up unwanted canes and replant.

If you only have room for one . . .

If space is tight, these varieties of classic fruit crops are guaranteed not to disappoint

Strawberry 'Mara de Bois'
Raspberry 'Malling Jewel'
Blackberry 'Oregon Thornless'
Blackcurrant 'Ben Connan'
Redcurrant 'Jonkheer van Tets'
Blueberry 'Sunshine Blue'
Fig 'Dauphine'
Apple 'King of the Pippins'
Pear 'Doyenne du Comice'
Plum 'Victoria'
Greengage 'Cambridge Gage'
Cherry 'Bigarreau Gaucher'
Quince 'Vranja'
Peach 'Avalon Pride'
Apricot 'Tomcot'
Rhubarb 'Timperley Early'

How to make New Plants for Free

Once you realise how easy it is to make your own plants, gardening becomes much less expensive – and a lot more fun. Plants are very biddable really; they want to multiply. Whether it's by dropping their seeds to sprout next year, sending out underground runners or forming new plantlets from a central crown, plants have one purpose in life: to live on in future generations.

This is very helpful to a gardener because it enables us to pilfer our friends' gardens for plants, seeds and cuttings without guilt. Obviously it would be bad manners to kill their plants in the process of doing this, so some basic skills need to be learned before you pounce on them. Propagating plants is straightforward, requiring nothing more than a sharp knife and a plastic bag. Before long your garden will be teeming with beautiful flowers, and each of the plants will have a story, reminding you of where they came from and the friends and relatives who gave them to you. Whether you're saving seed, splitting plants or snipping off a stem, the skills are easy to learn and invaluable. Give it a go and you'll never look back.

Seven easy ways to be a plant pilferer

1. Saving and collecting seed

Suitable for:
Sweet peas, nasturtiums, marigolds, hollyhocks, delphiniums, morning glory, cosmos, love-in-a-mist, rudbeckia, sunflowers, honesty, flowering tobacco, granny's bonnet, cornflowers, field poppies, Bupleurum, white lace flower, bishop's flower, corncockle.

Why buy packets of seeds every year when you can simply collect it from your own plants or those of your friends? So many popular garden plants can be grown this way and it is really satisfying to see the whole process through from tapping a dry seed head over a paper bag to watching the flower unfurl the following summer. The only seeds it's not worth saving are those from F1 hybrid varieties – if in doubt, this is clearly marked on the original seed packet, or you can look up the variety online. Plants that grow from F1 hybrid seed can be different from their parents, so you can't guarantee what you will get.

right Cut seed heads, such as these cornflowers, when dry and papery.

How to collect seed

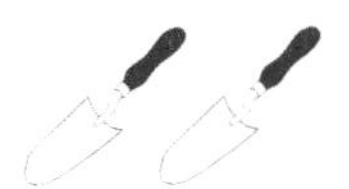

You will need
Secateurs
Dry seed heads
A paper bag or envelope
A tray

When to do it
Late summer to late autumn, when the flowers have turned brown and papery. In some plants, seedpods will rattle when you shake them.

How to do it
Using your secateurs, snip off the dry flower heads or seedpods and place them in a large paper bag or envelope. Take it inside and extract the seed, either simply by emptying the seedpod or rubbing the dead flower heads between your fingers. If you are left with a pile of seeds and chaff – bits of old seed case and petals – you can separate this by blowing gently over the surface of the mixture. The chaff is lighter so it tends to blow away. Alternatively, gather up the mixture in your fingers and sprinkle it onto the tray, blowing across it. When you have removed most of the chaff, you are ready to dry and store your seed.

How to dry and store seed

Seed has to be fully dry before storing, otherwise it can try to germinate or absorb moisture from the air and rot. Luckily, drying seed is very easy to do with stuff you probably already have in the kitchen.

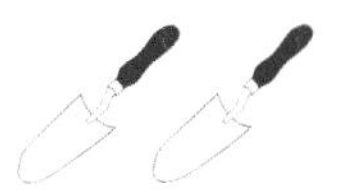

You will need
Dry rice
A baking tray
A jam jar with a lid
An old pair of tights
Seeds
A rubber band
Small plastic bag
Sticky label or indelible marker

When to do it
Late summer to mid-autumn

How to do it
Spread out the rice on the baking tray and bake in the oven at about 160°C for 45 minutes until it is bone dry. While still hot, pour the rice into the jam jar until it is about half-full and screw on the lid. Wait until the rice cools. Cut a foot off the tights and put your seeds into it, tying it up with the rubber band, then place this in the jar with the rice and screw the lid back on. Leave for a fortnight; during this time all the moisture will be sucked out of the seeds into the rice, making them completely dry and dormant. This prevents them germinating or rotting while you store them.

After this time you can simply put the seeds into a plastic bag where it will remain viable for several years. Don't forget to label it. Sow as usual in the spring.

far left Sprinkle the dry seed heads to separate the seed and chaff.
left Dry the seed before storing by placing in a jar with baked rice for a fortnight.

2. Transplanting self-sown seedlings

Suitable for:

Foxgloves, lady's mantle, *Verbena bonariensis*, verbascum, *Stipa tenuissima*, oregano, thyme.

Sometimes you don't even have to bother collecting seed because nature has already done the work for you. Many plants have a useful habit of dropping their seeds, which then germinate in the soil where they fell. All you have to do is enjoy them or dig them up and move them to your preferred spot. Most people don't need all these plants and weed them out, so they really won't mind if you ask to dig up a few from their garden.

You will need

A trowel

A small plastic pot

When to do it

Spring or autumn

How to do it

Hunt around the base of established plants for a small, mini version of itself. See theseedsite.co.uk for helpful identification images. Dig it up carefully, trying to get all of its roots along with the soil around them. Pop it into a small pot along with some more garden soil and replant it in when you get home, making sure you water it in well.

above House leeks, or sempervivums, constantly make new baby plants around their edges – simply pull one of these away from the parent and repot in gritty compost.

3. Taking offsets

Suitable for:

Sempervivum, echeveria, *Dicksonia antartica*

You will need

A pot
Horticultural grit
Free-draining, soil-based, potting compost such as John Innes No 2
An established plant that can be propagated by offsets

When to do it

Spring–autumn

How to do it

Fill the pot with a 50:50 mix of grit and compost. Look around the sides of a mature plant for a baby version and gently tug it away from the main plant, bringing its new roots with it. Then make a hole in the new compost and gently plant the offset. With sempervivum and echeveria you can fit up to eight new plants in a 20cm diameter pot. Dress the surface with more grit and water in well.

4. Taking root cuttings

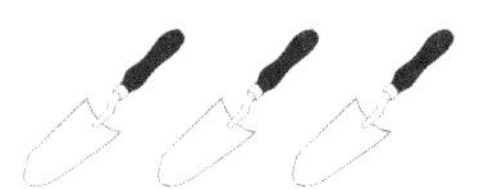

Suitable for:

Oriental poppy, globe thistle, bear's breeches, phlox, mint, Miss Willmott's ghost.

You will need

A garden fork
A sharp knife
Plastic pots to root your cuttings into – 9cm diameter ones are ideal
Soil-based compost such as John Innes No 2
Horticultural grit

When to do

Mid-autumn to late winter

How to do it

Dig around the outside of a plant to expose some of the thick white roots. If this isn't easy, just use your garden fork to lift the whole plant out of the ground, lay it on its side and have a good look at it. Using your sharp knife, cut off sections of the root. Never remove more than a third of the plant's root system or it might die. Replace the soil around the plant or replant it and water it well.

In the case of oriental poppies, globe thistle, Miss Wilmott's ghost and bear's breeches (*acanthus mollis* or *acanthus spinosa*), root cuttings will grow best if planted the right way up so make a flat cut at the top of the cutting and a slanted one at the bottom so you don't get confused. The top of the cutting is the end closest to the crown of the plant – you want the thick white ones, not the narrow ones. Cut your sections of root into 5cm lengths. Fill your plastic pots with compost and push a section of root into each one, with the slanted, cut end down, so the top is flush with the surface of the compost. Then cover with 1cm of grit (this reduces the chances of rot creeping in).

In the case of thinner roots such as those of phlox and mint, the technique is slightly different. Make the cuttings 10cm long, lay them horizontally on the surface of the compost and cover with 1cm of compost.

Water well and leave your potted cuttings outside in a sheltered spot (tucked up against the wall of the house will protect them from excessive rain). You should see new leaves emerging after a couple of weeks. If you have a greenhouse or cold frame they can overwinter in there, but if not, find a sheltered spot out of direct wind. In the spring you can plant them out in the garden.

above from left to right Use a sharp knife to cut a thick mint root into sections. Each section will soon sprout new shoots if laid on the surface of compost and then covered with a further 1cm layer of compost.

5. Layering

Climbers are some of the most expensive plants you can buy in the garden centre and, helpfully, two of our most popular are easy to propagate for nothing. You can easily increase your number of strawberry plants this way too.

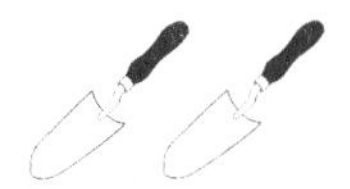

Suitable for:
Honeysuckle, clematis, strawberries.

You will need
An established honeysuckle, clematis or strawberry plant
A large plastic pot
Soil-based compost such as John Innes No 2
Secateurs
A trowel

When to do
Spring–autumn

How to do it
Find an established plant and look around the base where any long loose stems might be trailing along the ground. Give the stems an experimental tug to see if any have rooted into the soil, and if so, look for small plantlets. Carefully dig one up with as much of its roots as possible and sever it from the main plant. Then pot it up and take it home to replant.

If you can't find any rooted layered plants, simply make them yourself. Dig over an area of ground under the established plant then take a long stem and lay it along the soil. Bury it shallowly in several places along its length using the garden soil. Leave it for a few weeks then return to see if any of the sections you have buried have taken root. These can then be severed from the main plant and dug up for replanting.

right One mature strawberry plant can produce several 'babies' at the end of summer. Peg or weight these down to encourage them to root.

6. Stem cuttings

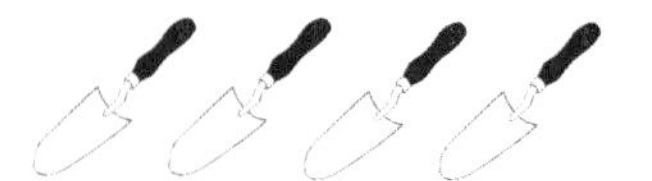

Suitable for:

Pelargoniums, rosemary, lavender, thyme, *Salvia nemorosa* 'Caradonna', aeoniums.

You will need

An established plant
A sharp knife and secateurs
Plastic pots about 7.5cm in diameter
Horticultural grit
Soil-based compost such as John Innes No 2

When to do

Either early–mid-spring or late summer–early autumn (or winter for aeoniums)

How to do it

Look for non-flowering shoots and with your knife or secateurs, remove them from the plant by making a straight cut just below a leaf, so you end up with a shoot around 10cm long. Next remove the lower leaves, leaving two to three leaves per cutting.

Fill the pots with a 50:50 mix of grit and compost, then make a hole in the centre and push the cutting in. Water well. Repeat so each cutting has its own pot. (Lavender and rosemary cuttings will benefit from a see-through plastic bag secured over the pot with an elastic band to increase the humidity.) Place the pots in a sheltered spot, such as a cold frame or tucked up against a shed or the house out of direct sun.

For aeoniums, the technique is slightly different. Cut a rosette with a 10cm piece of stem attached. Push this into the compost so the rosette is sitting on the surface and dress with grit. Water once only and then leave to establish indoors before putting outside in spring once all fear of frosts is over.

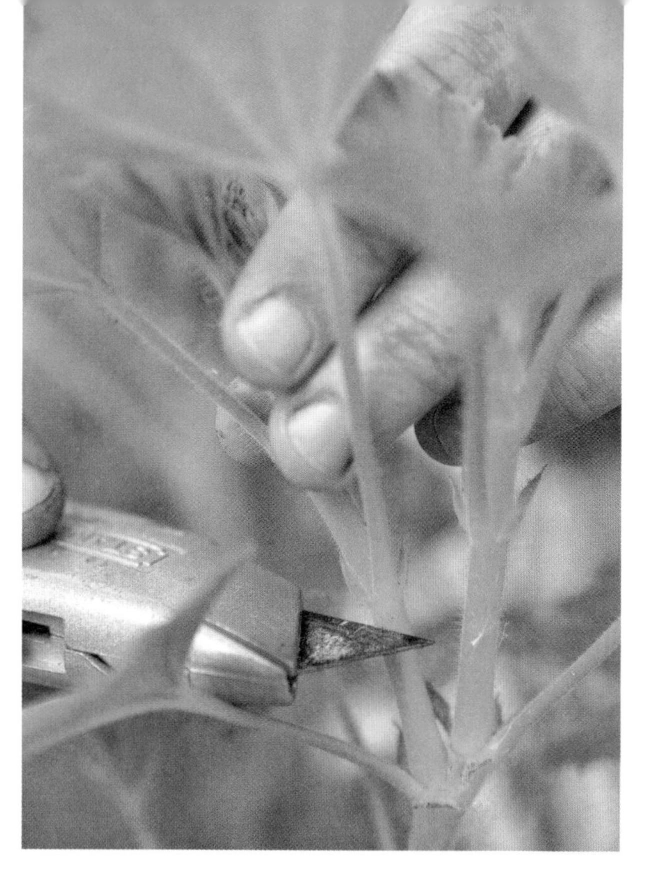

right Use a sharp, clean knife and cut a non-flowering shoot just below a leaf when taking pelargonium cuttings.

7. Division

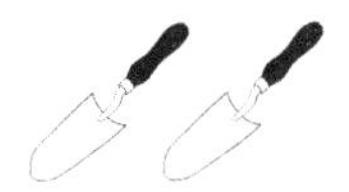

Suitable for:
Hardy geraniums, big blue lilyturf, wild ginger, alliums, Japanese anemone, silver grass, golden oats, feather reed grass, plum thistle, globe thistle, ice plant, *Salvia nemorosa* 'Caradonna', lamb's ears, Michaelmas daisy, hostas, chives, black bamboo.

You will need
An established plant
A hand fork or trowel
Plastic pots

When to do
Spring or autumn

How to do it
Look around the edges of an established clump – you're looking for plants that have developed there as the clump spread. You can spot them because they will have their own distinct centre. Using your trowel or fork, lift these plants, root and all, and gently tease them away from the main plant. Put them into a pot and cover their roots with garden soil. You can then plant it up in your own garden once you get home.

Since hostas have such dense root systems they should be divided by slicing them with a sharp knife (an old bread knife is ideal). In the case of black bamboo, dig up a clump and cut off the outer rhizomes. Cut these up so each piece of rhizome has at least one shoot, then pot them up with the rhizome just below the surface of the compost and the shoots exposed.

If there are no obvious plantlets, the plant has to be divided in a slightly different way. Large grasses should be dug up and then, using two garden forks placed back to back, levered apart to divide the root ball. Both sections can then be replanted.

Many plants, such as sedums (above) are resilient to being dug up and divided; just ensure you replant the parent plant carefully and water it well afterwards.

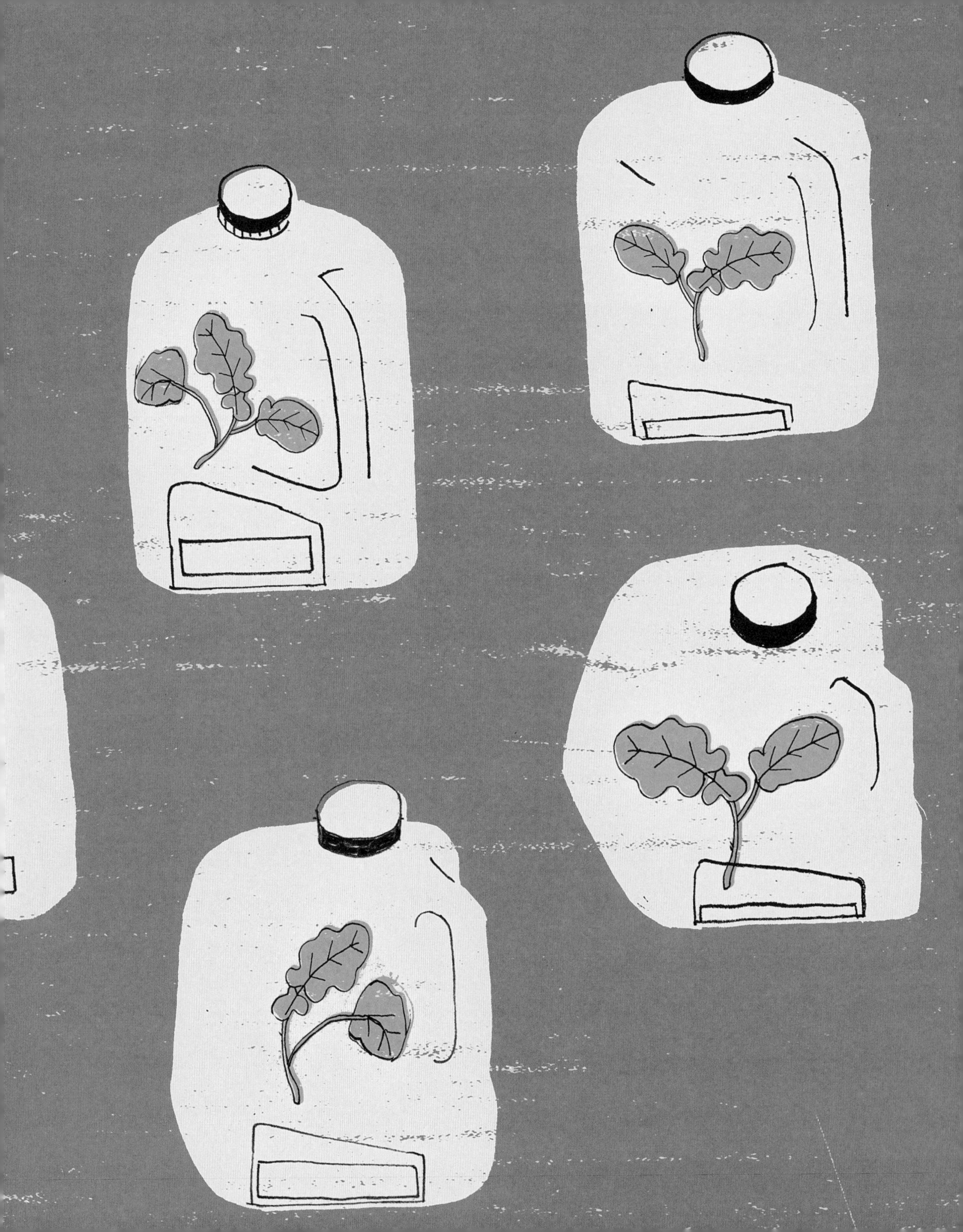

How not to Waste Money on Gardening Kit

The tools and equipment that go with gardening can be a hobby in themselves. If there's an activity in the garden – however specialised – chances are there is a tool for it. Whether it's giant claws to gather fallen leaves or perforated spouts to turn plastic bottles into watering cans, someone will have thought of it, moulded it in plastic and put a price tag on it. It's fun to wander the aisles of garden centres marvelling at the paraphernalia, but don't think you need to buy it all. Tools and equipment are the easiest way to splurge your money in the garden, and most of the time you'll find that ingenious piece of kit you bought gathering dust in the shed a year later.

Forget the rest: the 5 garden tools you can't do without

1. Hand trowel

For planting seedlings and getting out deep-rooted weeds.

2. Secateurs

For pruning and deadheading. Don't skimp on quality here, go for a high-end brand and you'll get a pair of secateurs will last you a decade or more. Choose bypass secateurs with blades that pass each other as they cut rather than anvil secateurs, which crush the stems.

3. Watering can

Make sure you get one with a rose attachment so you can gently water young seedlings without flooding or dislodging them.

4. Hoe

A Japanese razor hoe, or swoe, is ideal for most soils. The small, curved head means you can get into all those little gaps to cut weeds off at the base without damaging your precious plants – and it's light and sharp. A long-handled version will save your knees, while a short-handled one is ideal for raised beds and smaller borders.

5. Garden fork

This is the tool you need when digging over ground and planting or lifting larger plants. A garden spade is useful for digging large holes for trees and shrubs, but if it is one or the other, a fork is essential.

Make tools last longer by wiping with a rag dabbed with oil after using. Keep sharp with a sharpener stone or the sharpener you use for your carving knives. And don't leave them out in the rain.

Make your own pots for raising seedlings

When you grow vegetables or flowers from seed you can get through a lot of little plastic pots. They are not particularly expensive and can be used again year after year, of course, but you'll need somewhere to store them when they are not in use and you should also clean them every time you reuse them to prevent the spread of moulds and diseases.

If you make your own pots from newspaper or cardboard you won't have to clean them or buy them, and they are so ridiculously easy to make, there's just no reason not to do it! Once your plant is big enough, simply plant it out, pot and all (the cardboard or paper will biodegrade naturally into the soil), or unwrap the root ball from the paper.

The only thing to remember when growing in cardboard or paper pots is that you should water them from below – watering from above can encourage moulds to build up on the pot. Tightly pack your pots into a watertight tray or old cake tin and pour water into the container so that the compost soaks it up from below.

Make pots out of newspaper

Free, easy and quick to make, pots made from newspapers are great either for starting off seeds or for transplanting seedlings into.

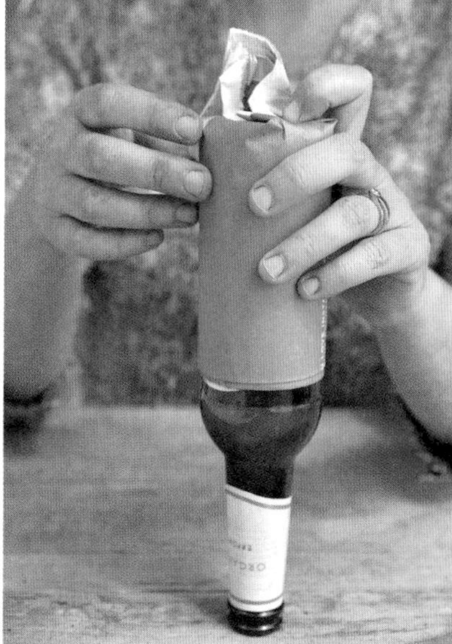

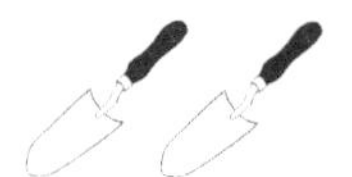

You will need

Newspaper – tabloid size is ideal
A bottle or tin can, depending on how big you want your pot
Multipurpose, peat-free compost
Seeds or seedlings

When to do it

Spring

How to do it

Open your tabloid size newspaper to the centre pages and remove the centre spread. If it is stapled, remove it carefully because you don't want holes in your pot. Fold the paper together again then lay it on a table in front of you and fold it in half lengthways, making a tight crease with your fingers.

Lay the paper diagonally in front of you with the folded side nearest you. Then take your bottle or can and lay it on the end of the paper nearest you, leaving about a third of the paper out – this will become the bottom of the pot.

Hold the bottom of the paper securely against the bottle and begin rolling the paper until it is completely wrapped around the bottle. Now turn it upside down and, still with the bottle inside, fold the newspaper that's sticking out down to make the bottom of the pot. There is no science to this bit, it's just a question of scrunching down the excess paper. Now turn the pot upright and push it down on the table, hard, so that the bottle flattens the bottom of the pot before carefully extracting the bottle. You now have a pot that can be filled with compost and sown as usual.

above and right Newspaper pots are best watered from below to avoid creating excessively damp conditions around the base of the seedling, which can lead to damping off (see page 155). Pack them into a tray or tin lid and simply pour a few centimetres of water into the container.

Freecycle and other swap websites are a great source of used gardening equipment, from sheds to greenhouses, pots to tools. Sign up to your local group and see what's on offer.

Make pots out of kitchen-roll tubes

The inner tubes of kitchen or toilet rolls make instant pots and are particularly good for seeds that like a long root run, such as sweet peas or beans. Sow direct into the tubes and then plant the whole thing out when the plant has matured.

You will need
Inner tubes from kitchen or toilet rolls
Multipurpose, peat-free compost
Seeds

When to do it
Spring

How to do it
If you're using a kitchen-roll inner tube, first cut it in half horizontally so you end up with two tubes. If you are using a toilet roll, there's no need to do this. You then need to fold one end of the tube upwards to stop compost falling out. To do this, simply make four tears about a centimetre long around the outside of one end and fold the flaps up and inwards to make the bottom of the pot. You can now fill the pot with compost and sow as normal.

Make free plant labels

It's always worth labelling seeds as you sow them – not only so that you later remember what variety they are but also when you sowed them. You can buy plastic, wooden or even fancy slate labels for the purpose, but why bother? Simply cut up any plastic container – a yoghurt pot, plastic bottle, etc. – and write on it with an indelible marker, then push it into the compost. Job done.

Wonderful willow: why you don't need to buy wigwams, arches and other plant supports

Willow is a fantastic material to use in the garden because it's cheap, bendy and very strong. Runner-bean wigwams, cloches, tunnels and even children's play huts can all be made with surprisingly little effort and creating them is great fun. They give your garden real individuality and charm and, since willow is a sustainable crop you won't be costing the environment anything. If you're lucky enough to have willow growing in yours or a friend's garden, you can just cut stems down to the ground and use them, but it's also very easy to buy willow online from a specialist supplier who will deliver it to your home in the quantity and length you need. An online search should reveal some suppliers relatively local to you. A bundle or two will go a very long way for little in the way of cash outlay. If you can find local willow you will save yourself the delivery cost too.

Which willow should I buy?

If you are making a garden structure that you don't want to be rooted in the ground, brown willow is the one to go for. When looking online it's worth getting your head round a few 'willow' terms so you know what to buy.

A length of willow is known as a 'rod'. You buy rods in 'bundles'. 'Living willow' and 'green willow' are wood that has just been cut, so they are very bendy and will sprout if you push the rods into the ground. Living willow differs from green willow in that it is chosen from varieties that are particularly strong growing and disease resistant, which makes them better for garden structures. Living willow is fantastic for green screens to hide compost bins or children's trampolines. It is, however, only available for planting during winter and up to mid-spring.

'Brown willow' is wood that has been cut months previously and allowed to dry out. It is available year round and is cheaper than living willow. This wood will not sprout if pushed into the ground but it does need soaking before use to make it more flexible, because it is nothing like as bendy as the green kind. Soak it for one day per foot of length, i.e. a seven-foot-long willow wand will need soaking for seven days. You can, however, buy it pre-soaked but you will then need to use it within about three days or it will dry out again.

Many willow suppliers sell affordable 'soaking bags'; basically long plastic bags you fill with water and push the rods into. Tie up the end and you have a watertight bag. Alternatively, you can soak your willow in the bath if it's short enough – although you may need your bath in the meantime! Pond liner can also be fashioned into a trough fairly easily if you prop up the sides with bricks, boxes, logs or other sturdy structures and fill with water.

If you have room, why not root a few living willow rods to start your own plantation? That way you won't have to buy it again and can harvest your own for any structures you want to build.

How much willow should I buy?

One 1kg bundle of brown willow will contain about 100 rods, which is ideal for various small garden projects. Any willow you don't want to use can simply be stored dry. A plant wigwam will use around 13 rods, a cloche about 10. If you want to make a kid's play hut (see page 74), you'll need about 45.

What length of willow should I choose?

It depends what you're using it for. Consider how tall you want the structure to be and then add about 15cm to allow for the ends to be pushed into the ground. Willow rods have a thick end, tapering to a narrow point.

Make a simple willow wigwam for beans, peas, sweet peas or tomatoes

This wigwam is ideal for any climbing plant and looks particularly good with runner beans, sweet peas or edible peas clambering up it. You can, of course, buy no end of willow wigwams from garden centres, but why would you when making them yourself is a fraction of the price? Make your own and you'll end up with something individual and natural-looking that you can use for up to five years before the wood splinters.

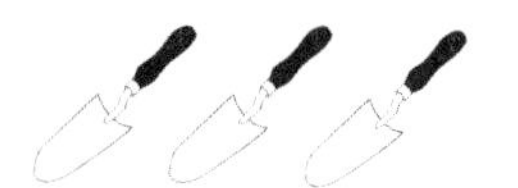

You will need

13 x 180cm brown willow rods (pre-soaked, see page 126). If willow is not available, use any other flexible wood such as hazel or dogwood

Garden twine

Secateurs

When to do it

Year round

If growing cordon tomatoes on your willow wigwam, ensure you keep pinching out the sideshoots to prevent the wigwam becoming top-heavy and unstable.

How to do it

Decide how big you want the base of your wigwam to be and draw a rough circle in the soil with a stick – you need to make this in situ. Take seven rods and push them into the ground to a depth of about 10cm, evenly spacing them around the circumference of the circle. Then tie the tops of the rods together with twine to make a wigwam, trying to make the tying point as near the centre of the circle as possible.

Next take two more rods. Depending on how flexible they are (test by seeing if you can make a rough circle without the wood snapping), cut off 50–80cm of the thickest end so you are left with only the more flexible, thinner section. You can use the offcuts to prop up garden plants or seedlings. Tie the thick ends together tightly with garden twine. Position one rod on either side of one of the uprights towards the base of the wigwam and pull them so the tying point is snug against the upright. Tie this to the upright. You can now begin weaving your rods around the wigwam upwards in a loose spiral, twisting the rods round themselves between uprights and either side of each upright to make a strong structure. As you get to the top of the wigwam, push the thin ends through the top knot to make it secure. Repeat this twice, each time using two rods and weaving upwards in a spiral but taking a different base point so you have roughly evenly spaced spirals. Tie off any sticking-out willow or obvious twine and your wigwam is ready for its plants.

right Soaked willow is bendy enough to weave into a spiral structure. Push the base of the rods down against the edge if the container to keep the structure strong.

Make a free cloche to protect plants

You can spend a lot on garden cloches, from the relatively affordable plastic domes to high-end glass affairs, but you can easily make a cloche yourself that will cost just pennies and will protect young plants from wind, dogs, rabbits and birds. If you staple horticultural fleece around the structure you can keep vulnerable plants warm in winter; or you can staple insect mesh to it to keep out caterpillars, aphids and carrot fly.

You will need

10 willow rods, either brown soaked willow or a mixture of brown (for the main structure) and green (for weaving). If you can't find green willow, use any flexible stems such as brambles (with the spines rubbed off)
Secateurs
Garden twine or plastic ties
Scissors

When to do it

Any time of year

How to do it

This cloche is made in situ, so first decide where you want it to go. Push the thick end of one of the brown willow rods into the ground and bend it over to make a hoop, pushing the thinner end into the ground. Cut off as much of the thin end as necessary to get the size of hoop you want. Repeat this with the two other rods until you have a simple dome-like structure.

Next, take two rods of green willow (or thin, flexible brown willow), place the thick ends either side of an upright and tie them securely to it. Twist the rods around themselves, weaving around either side of the next upright and continuing until you have made a ring around the cloche. Repeat with another pair of rods, starting from a different upright. Once you are happy with this ring, start making another one towards the top of the cloche. You can make as many woven rings as you want. Tie in any whippy ends with twine.

from top down Push two rods into the ground to make a basic dome; tie horizontal rods either side of the uprights; weave them around the uprights to make hoops that strengthen the structure.

Do I need to buy a raised bed kit?

If you want to grow vegetables and are absolutely sure you need a raised bed (see page 98), you can either buy a ready-prepared kit or construct one yourself. There are plenty of kits out there, ranging from the affordable to the luxury, that will last many years, but many tend to be rather small, requiring you to buy more than one, and even the most convenient of them will require you to put them together. If you're not careful the costs soon add up and the carrots and broccoli you are growing start looking like luxury food items you may as well have flown in individually!

If you've decided to make your own raised beds from scratch the basic construction is pretty much the same whatever materials you use. You'll need four short posts to hammer into the ground to form the corners and four lengths of wood or other material for the sides. Simply screw or nail the sides to the four posts.

It will save you money as well as hassle and time to make fewer larger beds than lots of small ones. It will also be much easier if you make your bed a simple rectangular shape rather than a fancy octagon or whatever. As long as you can easily reach into the centre of the bed without stepping on the soil, the shape and dimensions don't really matter. Remember to leave at least 45cm between beds so you can easily get around between them.

Before you decide which to go for, remember, if you are placing your raised bed on hard standing such as concrete, make sure it's at least 45cm deep so plant roots can spread out. If you're constructing a bed on top of garden soil, 20–30cm deep sides are ideal, although you need to allow for the fact that 2–3cm of the board may be buried underground for stability.

Savvy tip

If you are making a raised bed in an area of grass, dig up the turf and turn it upside down and bury it in the lower level of the raised bed so that it will rot down and enrich the soil.

Make your own raised beds: the options

Scrap timber

Pros: Free

Cons: If the wood is not treated with preservative it may not last more than three or four years. Requires some sawing.

Preservative treated timber or scaffolding boards

Pros: Very sturdy, attractive, long-lasting, easy to weed and maintain.

Cons: Unless you can get hold of free or budget second-hand scaffolding boards, treated wood can be surprisingly expensive. Creosoted wood should be avoided since it could leach dangerous chemicals into the soil.

Hazel and willow

Pros: Cheap, attractive.

Cons: Will only last about four years, takes some time to make (see page 132 for how), weeds can be a problem growing through the woven edges.

Bricks/stones

Pros: Cheap/free, can look attractive.

Cons: Unless you use mortar you can only really stack two bricks without them becoming unstable, so the bed will be relatively shallow (12cm). Weeds tend to be a problem growing up in the cracks and slugs and snails will hide there.

Extra-large builders' bags

Pros: Cheap, instant, deep enough for large plants.

Cons: Not particularly attractive unless you surround them with flexible willow screening.

Build a raised bed from hazel and willow

If you are lucky enough to have access to growing hazel and willow, you can make raised beds for free. Willow can also be bought very affordably online. The end result is rustic, natural and charming, and making these beds is great fun too. For more on willow see Wonderful willow on page 126.

You will need

Hazel sticks (or any wood) at least 5cm thick and as straight as possible (don't use green willow for the posts or it may root)
Tape measure
Saw
Stanley knife
Mallet
Secateurs
An armful of willow rods at least as long as the longest sides of your raised bed
Pond liner, strong black plastic or weed suppressing membrane (optional)
Scissors (optional)

When to do it

Green willow, the most flexible, is available from winter to mid-spring. Brown willow is less flexible but is available all year round and can be soaked to make it more flexible for weaving (see page 126).

How to do it

Saw the hazel into 10–12 sections, depending on how big your bed will be; each section needs to be roughly 30cm long. Then sharpen one end with your Stanley knife to make a pointed stake. Using the mallet, hammer the stakes into the ground to make the perimeter of the raised bed, spacing them as equally as possible.

Take one of your willow rods and place the thicker end inside one of the corner posts. Be sure not to push any end of green willow into the ground since it may root. Then begin weaving it in and out of the other posts.

If you are using green willow it may be flexible enough to weave around the corners of the beds so you can continue until the rod 'runs out', at which point simply proceed with a new one. If you are using much less flexible brown willow, build up each side one rod at a time, cutting the rods at the corners with secateurs. Work your way around all four sides in turn before adding the second layer.

This time weave around the uprights in the alternate direction to create a strong structure. Keep building up the layers, gently pushing the willow rods down as you go to reduce gaps between them, until you near the top of the posts.

Lining the bed is not essential but it will prolong its life. Weed suppressing membrane will keep weeds from invading through the gaps in the willow. Pond liner or other strong black plastic will not only keep out weeds but also keep the willow dry. It's not necessary to line the base of the bed; simply cut a strip slightly wider than the height of the raised bed sides and line the inside edges.

Now fill the bed with top soil and you are ready to plant.

Savvy tip

Topsoil is expensive to buy since it is so heavy. If you can take topsoil from other areas of the garden that don't need it – such as paths – to fill the raised bed it would save you money. You can then fill the paths with bark chips, which are relatively cheap and much lighter to carry.

Do I need a greenhouse?

A greenhouse is invaluable for the keen gardener. With a greenhouse, the range of plants you can grow expands suddenly and the world is your oyster. You can start off your vegetables earlier, protect cuttings and other propagated plants over the winter and grow tender plants that would die unprotected outside. You'll get a decent crop of aubergines and sweet peppers and, not to be discounted, you'll save every windowsill in your house from being covered with seedlings in plant pots from early spring onwards.

But there's a catch, of course. Greenhouses don't come cheap. A top-end greenhouse will cost you more than a luxury family holiday. Even a not terribly attractive, budget greenhouse – made from frosted polycarbonate, not glass – will cost you about the price of a garden shed.

If you are not prepared to stump up for a greenhouse, there is an alternative. A cold frame will also keep your plants dry, snug and protected over winter. It can be used to start off early sowings and is a handy place to put tender perennials such as pelargoniums over winter.

Build a very affordable cold frame

If you are lucky enough to have some old bricks somewhere, this is a great use for them. If not, any builders' merchants will have budget ones that you can buy inexpensively. Twin-walled polycarbonate is highly affordable, lasts years and can be bought online – simply enter your measurements and they will cut it for you.

You will need

Bricks

A sheet of twin-walled polycarbonate

When to do it

All year round; or you can make this temporarily for your spring seedlings and put the materials back in the shed afterwards to make space

How to do it

Simply lay out your bricks to the same dimensions as your sheet of polycarbonate. Build up the walls, making the front wall at least two bricks lower than the one at the back. Add another stack of bricks in the back middle for stability, then pop the sheet on top, weighing it down with a couple of bricks to stop the wind blowing it off.

right The ideal place to build a cold frame is against a warm, sheltered wall.

Either leave the cold frame in situ all year or simply unstack the bricks and store when not in use to save space.

Keep Your Garden Healthy for [Almost] Nothing

'Look after your soil and the plants look after themselves.' It's a much-quoted mantra but one that makes very good sense. Most soils benefit from the addition of well-rotted organic matter in the form of garden compost. Plants – particularly hungry ones, such as vegetable crops – really do need it. It improves soil drainage so plant roots don't get waterlogged and enriches the soil with nutrients.

You can use well-rotted farmyard manure or spent farmyard compost if you have easy access to it, but for most of us the best way to ensure a constant supply of organic matter for our garden is to make it ourselves in the compost bin. Making garden compost is a no-brainer: it's easy, it's free and it makes your garden grow. It can even cut down your kitchen waste and will save you the hassle of carting bags of lawn clippings through the house to get rid of. It's recycling in the best possible way.

Your garden prunings, lawn mowings and kitchen scraps will, over a period of around six months to a year, break down into rich, dark, crumbly stuff the colour of chocolate sponge. Just spread it on your beds in spring or autumn and let the worms take it down. A mulch of garden compost retains moisture in the soil and will keep weeds down too.

You don't need a bin to make compost; if space allows you could just pile up your old leaves, lawn clippings and banana peels in a big heap – they would break down eventually. But if you don't want decomposing food and vegetation spilling out onto your lawn you'll want to contain your compost in something.

Beg before you buy: bin for free

Check with your local authority to see if they are giving away compost bins to residents. They often have a supply of plastic bins they can deliver for free.

How to make your own compost bin

You can buy compost bins from any garden centre or online supplier; plastic, wood, round, square, tumbling, static – there is a bin for everyone. Some, particularly the wooden slatted sort you fit together yourself, can be good value if you search around online. Solid wooden ones are good quality, longer lasting and will keep the compost moister, but they're not cheap. Either way, you can at least halve your costs if you make your own bin.

There are several ways to do this – using planks, discarded pallets or bricks nailed onto corner posts to make a box – and the internet is full of tutorials. These methods, however, are perhaps the quickest and easiest.

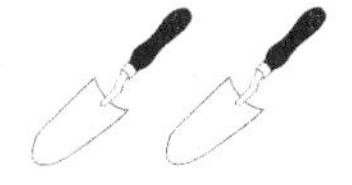

You will need

4 tree stakes
A sledgehammer or post-hole digger, depending on how hard your ground is
1 roll of plastic mesh netting 1 x 4m
Garden shears
Plastic stretchy string such as Flexi-Tie or plastic cable ties (garden twine won't last)
An 80 x 80cm piece of plastic pond liner, old carpet, thick cardboard or strong plastic to keep the bin insulated and most of the rain out

How to do it

Find a suitable spot for your compost bin; it needs to be placed on soil or grass, so avoid hard-standing areas such as paving or concrete. Hammer the stakes into the ground to make a square 80 x 80cm. If your ground is very hard, a post-hole digger is useful here. Then unroll the mesh and fold it in half. Cut along the fold with your shears so you have two 2m pieces. Fold each of these in half again and cut so you have four 1m squares of mesh. Using the cable ties or string, tie the mesh securely to the corner stakes, tying at the top, middle and bottom of each stake to avoid it sagging too much. Trim off any excess mesh with your shears. Once you begin to fill your bin, place the plastic, carpet or cardboard on top of the compost material every time you add it to keep excess rain out.

Every couple of months you'll want to turn your compost to speed up the decomposition. To access it, just snip through some of the ties to fold back one side of the mesh. Once you have turned the compost you can simply tie up the mesh again.

What to put in your compost bin

Yes

Uncooked fruit and vegetable peelings and waste
Torn-up cardboard (hand-sized pieces)
Eggshells (wash them first so they don't attract rats)
Lawn clippings (add these in layers interspersed with torn-up cardboard to avoid a bulk or they can get slimy)
Garden prunings
Any twigs or branches thinner than your finger, chopped into pieces

No

Cooked fruit and vegetable waste
Meat, fish, eggs or dairy
Branches or twigs thicker than your finger
Flowering weeds – they'll set seed in your bin and you'll just reintroduce them to the garden
Perennial weeds – they can re-root in the bin and just keep on growing. See Feed with Weeds (page 145) for a savvier way to deal with them.

Whatever bin you choose, don't bother buying or making a compost bin much smaller than $80cm^2$ and 1m high. Anything smaller than that and the compost will take too long to break down.

right For an even cheaper, if shorter-term solution, you can use bamboo screening to make a compost bin that will blend naturally into most garden settings. Bamboo is naturally water-resistant so will last a couple of years. This inexpensive material is sold in all DIY and garden stores as a screen or windbreak. Just unroll a length of it and wrap it around four stakes as above, tying it securely with plastic stretchy string or cable ties as you go.

Wormeries

If you don't have space for a regular compost bin, you can still create compost to keep your plants healthy thanks to the wonderful powers of worms. Wormeries are great for small gardens, balconies or roof terraces since they not only take up very little room (they're about a fifth of the size of a regular compost bin) but they also don't need to be placed on the soil surface, so they are ideal for paved or concrete areas. They will produce compost much faster than a normal compost bin too – within three months you can have fantastic, rich, crumbly brown compost that's perfect for digging into your garden soil or plant pots. A little goes a long way with this potent fertiliser.

Wormeries are fascinating too. It's somewhere between having a compost bin and a very low-maintenance pet; you feed your worms little and often and watch them work away converting your kitchen scraps and bits of discarded cardboard into wonderful plant food.

Beg before you buy: worms

The best place to find worms for your new wormery is in someone else's established wormery. They'll not only be free but healthy, and, if you take some of the compost too, they'll have ready-made bedding to settle into in their new home. If you have a friend with a healthy population, ask if they'd mind if you have some of their worms. You'll need at least 200 worms to start off with – a couple of handfuls should do it along with as much of their bedding material as your friend will let you walk off with. Pop the worms in a tub or bucket and tip them out into your new wormery when you get home.

How to make a wormery

You can easily buy wormery kits online, but they tend to be quite expensive. Luckily, you can make one yourself at a fraction of the cost since all you really need is a plastic storage box with a lid, which is easy to find in any homeware or thrift store.

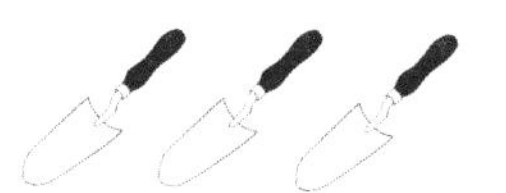

You will need

1 plastic crate or box – around 50cm long and wide and 25cm deep – with a lid
1 power drill with 2.5–5mm drill bit
2 bricks or similar to stand it on
Cardboard – old boxes are ideal
Worm bedding – either from an existing wormery, garden compost or well-rotted farmyard manure (if you buy worms online they usually come with bedding)
500g composting worms, either from an existing wormery (see opposite), online supplier or fishing-tackle shop. Buy either tiger worms (aka brandling or *Eisenia fetida*) or Dendrobaena worms (aka the European night crawler or *Eisenia hortensis*)
Kitchen scraps

How to do it

First, drill about 15 holes in the base of the crate or box. This is important since worms need air to survive. Then drill another 10 or so holes in the sides of the box towards the top. Avoid drilling holes in the lid itself because that will let in rain. Decide on a location for your wormery somewhere out of direct sunlight – behind a garden shed is ideal – and sit it on a couple of bricks or blocks. This also improves ventilation.

Next cut a piece of cardboard the same size as the box and place it in the base of the box. Sprinkle it with water. If you are using a clear plastic box it's important that you make it opaque since worms dislike daylight. Cut pieces of cardboard to fit and slot them down each side of the box on the inside so it is dark inside. Then add a

1. Line the base of the box with cardboard and sprinkle with water.
2. Line the sides with cardboard too if it's a clear box.
3–4. Gently tip the worms onto a layer of worm compost or garden compost.
5. Add a couple of handfuls of chopped raw fruit and vegetables.
6. Add torn up cardboard.
7. Lay a piece of cardboard over the compost then replace lid and move the box to a sheltered spot out of direct sun. Place on bricks to let excess water drain out.

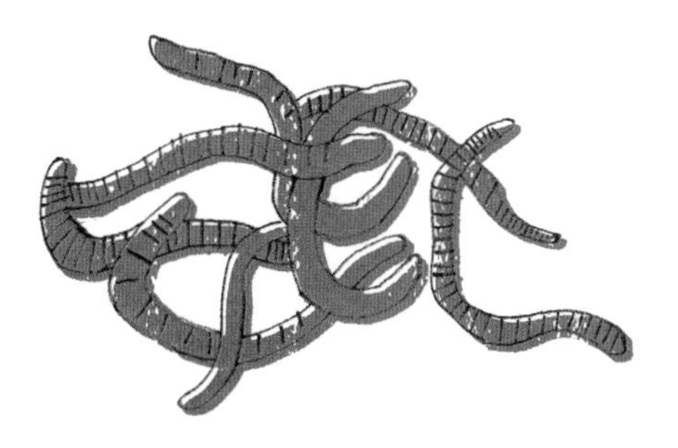

3–5cm layer of bedding for your worms – either from an established wormery or use well-rotted garden compost. Carefully tip out your worms then add kitchen scraps – the equivalent of a banana, an apple and a carrot all chopped up is about the right quantity to start off with. Sprinkle this on the surface and then cover with another piece of cardboard to keep everything moist. Replace the lid.

Savvy tip

Make your pots persevere. Worm compost is particularly useful for container gardeners since it can enliven old compost in your pots. As any balcony or windowsill grower knows, it's always a bit of a conundrum knowing what to do with compost in pots when you've finished harvesting a crop as it's usually full of roots and rather dry. Rather than chucking it away and buying new compost, just sift out the roots with your fingers (and add these to the wormery), then mix in a couple of handfuls of worm compost to each pot. You can then use the refreshed compost for flowering plants or less hungry crops such as salads, carrots or peas. Be aware that heavy feeding crops such as tomatoes, potatoes, peppers and courgettes should really have new compost each time, though.

Looking after your wormery

Feed your worms little and often, chopping up the food you give them so they can eat it. A new wormery is easily overwhelmed by too much food, so as a general guide to quantity, aim to give them the equivalent of one banana, the grounds from your breakfast coffee, a couple of apple cores and a torn-up A4-sized piece of cardboard per day to start with. As the worms settle and the colony grows, you can add more. After a while you will get to know your worms and be able to gauge how much food they can cope with.

What do you feed your worms?

Worms will eat any raw fruit or vegetable scraps (though citrus fruits and onions are too acidic for them, so avoid these) and small amounts of cooked foods such as pasta, but avoid fatty foods, fish and meat. Tea bags and coffee grounds can go in too. Crushed eggshells are also good since they provide grit, which the worms need, and reduce acidity. Worms love cardboard so will happily chomp through packaging and the inner tubes of your kitchen roll if you tear it up first into matchbox-sized pieces. Do the same with newspaper. Aim to add around half food waste to half cardboard/newspaper. If the wormery starts to smell, you're probably overfeeding the worms so the food is rotting before they can eat it. Remove the food and start again with smaller quantities.

Harvesting the compost

After about three months, some of the compost should be ready to use. Scrape off the top half with a trowel and put it in a bin bag temporarily. This top half is where the vast majority of the worms will be living and you don't want to remove them with the compost. Then harvest the bottom half of the compost and dig it into your garden soil or pots. Don't worry if there are still a few worms in it – they'll do your soil good. One handful will revitalise tired compost in a 30cm diameter pot or give a garden plant a boost if dug in around it. Be sure to dig in the compost rather than leave it on the soil surface since it tends to become hard if left to dry out. Then return the contents of the bin bag to the wormery to continue their composting.

Make your own plant feeds

So we know how to feed the soil, but many plants, especially fruit and vegetables, really benefit from a bit of extra feeding now and then to keep them in good health. Shop-bought plant feeds can be expensive and are often based on man-made chemicals, but you really don't need to buy them when it's so easy to make your own liquid plant food.

Nettles can be nice

Stinging nettles make a feed that's high in nitrogen, the element that promotes leafy growth, so it's good for salads, spinach and other leafy crops, as well as garden plants. There's something particularly satisfying about turning a plant that can sting you into something useful.

For a basic nettle feed just cut two or three good-sized armfuls of nettles, scrunch them up and soak them in a bucket of water for a couple of weeks. Then strain off the liquid – beware, it really stinks – and dilute it until it's the colour of weak black tea (usually about 1 part nettle brew to 10 parts water). You can then water this around your crops. It makes a good lawn feed, too, since it's high in nitrogen – the element that promotes green growth. Water this on your lawn with a watering can in spring for a green boost.

Savvy tip

Feed with weeds. All garden weeds can be used to make plant feed in the same way. Flowering annual weeds shouldn't be added to your compost bin because their seeds can remain in the compost and either sprout there or germinate once you've added the compost back to the soil. Similarly, persistent weeds such as dock, nettles and brambles shouldn't be added to the compost heap because they tend to re-root and keep growing. Instead, soak weeds such as these in a bucket of water for a couple of weeks. You'll kill them thoroughly, with the added benefit that you'll end up with a nutrient-rich plant food that you can dilute in the same way as the nettle feed.

above Cut the top third of nettle plants and don't forget long gloves.

Make a mini nettle feed factory

If making nettle feed in a bucket offends your nostrils too much, this is a great way to produce less smelly, concentrated nettle feed in a small space – ideal propped up behind a shed or other out-of-the-way spot. You can save the concentrate in glass jars for up to a month before using. This contraption also works for comfrey (see page 148).

You will need

1 large plastic bottle
Scissors or a craft knife
A jam jar with lid
Gloves
Stinging nettles
A stick
A stone to weigh the nettles down

When to do it

Spring–summer

How to do it

Cut the bottom off your plastic bottle with scissors or a knife. Take the lid off the jam jar and store it somewhere safe, then push the bottle, narrow end down, into the jar. Wearing gloves, cut some nettles, scrunch them up and push them into the bottle, using the stick to push them tightly as far as they will go. Then weigh them down with the stone. Prop up the whole contraption against a wall or in a corner, to stop the bottle toppling off, and leave.

After a couple of weeks, a dark liquid will start to drip out of the bottle into the jar. Once you have enough liquid, screw the lid back on and replace with another jar. You can add new nettles whenever there is space. The nettle concentrate will keep for at least a month in the jar – simply dilute it to the colour of weak black tea and water it onto your plants.

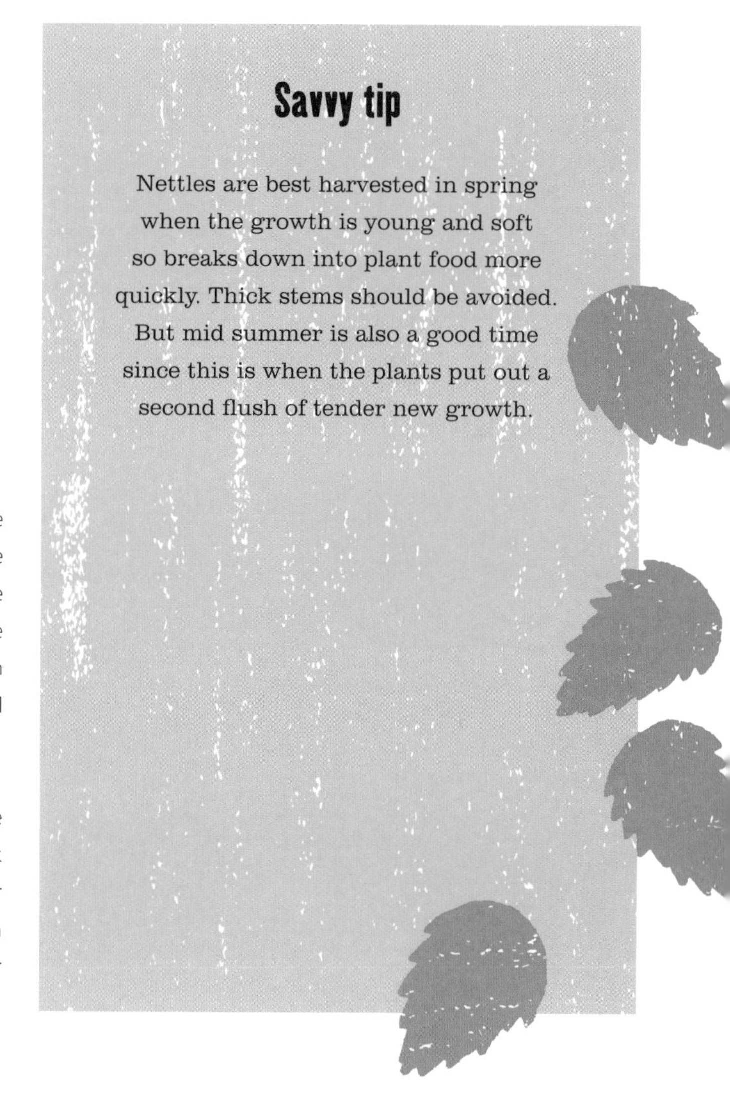

Savvy tip

Nettles are best harvested in spring when the growth is young and soft so breaks down into plant food more quickly. Thick stems should be avoided. But mid summer is also a good time since this is when the plants put out a second flush of tender new growth.

right Ensure you squash the leaves in tight and apply pressure from a stone or brick since you want the leaves to rot down rather than dry out.

Get comfy with comfrey

Arguably the most effective home-made plant food comes from comfrey, a leafy plant that every organic gardener should find space for in the garden. Comfrey has a particularly deep tap root (up to 3m long) which can access soil nutrients other plants can't reach and bring them up into its leaves. We can then access these nutrients by cutting the leaves and letting them break down to release the chemicals into the soil around our plants. Just one comfrey plant can produce 10kg of leaves a year.

Comfrey contains two to three times the potassium levels of farmyard manure and this makes it particularly useful for flowering and fruiting plants, which need this element for successful growth. Tomatoes, potatoes, peppers, aubergines, sweetcorn, pumpkins, courgettes and other heavy-feeding fruiting plants will particularly benefit from a twice-weekly feed in the growing season, but garden flowers will also enjoy a fortnightly feed too. Either just pick the leaves and lay them on the ground around your plants to rot down and release their nutrients or make a liquid feed from them.

How to grow comfrey

Buy (or 'Beg before you buy', see right) a handful of comfrey plants, find them a quiet corner and they'll grow happily for up to 20 years. Make sure you use Russian comfrey, 'Bocking 14', since the wild comfrey tends to self-seed all over the place. These plants are happy in sun or partial shade, so they are perfect for planting near your compost bins or around the garden shed. Bees love the flower too. Space the plants about 60cm apart and keep the area weeded as they establish. If you plant in the autumn you could be harvesting by summer. If planting in spring, you'll be harvesting by the following spring.

You can harvest comfrey plants four to five times a year. In mid-spring, cut the whole plant to 5cm off the ground with shears or secateurs and gather the leaves. Wear gloves because the leaves and stems are covered in irritating hairs. Then leave the plants to recover for four to five weeks before making another cut. You can then make two further cuts at five-week intervals, but don't cut any later than early autumn so that the plants can build up strength for the subsequent year.

far right Comfrey leaves contain little fibre so break down into liquid food very easily. You can harvest comfrey four to five times a year.

Beg before you buy: comfrey

If you're lucky enough to know someone who already grows comfrey you can get free plants very easily. It's best to do this in early to mid-spring. Find an established plant and drive a garden spade horizontally under it, about 8cm below the surface of the soil, severing the plant – the crown – from its roots. Cover the cut roots of the original plant with soil and it will regrow within a couple of months.

Split the crown up into several offsets – it is easy to see where to divide the clump because it will naturally have split into mini crowns, each with their own central growing point. Using secateurs, cut through the main root to create separate crowns, each with 5–10cm sections of root. You should get at least six offsets per plant. Cut off any leaves to about 5cm from the growing point, since the transplanted crown will not be able to sustain them. Put the offsets in a plastic bag to keep them damp and replant them in your garden as soon as possible, about 60cm apart, so that the cut leaf stems are just above the soil surface.

Make a comfrey feed drainpipe

Comfrey makes a fantastic, potassium-rich, liquid plant food which is great for crops such as tomatoes and any flowering plants too. The real benefit of this rather Heath-Robinson plant-food contraption is that it won't take up much space and can easily be installed behind a garden shed where you won't see it. Since it makes concentrate rather than diluted feed – as some other methods do – the resulting liquid tends to smell rather less too. All you have to do is to push comfrey leaves into the top of the pipe and wait for concentrated plant food to drip out of the bottom into a container. You then dilute this to use on your plants at a ratio of about 40:1 – about a capful in a watering can. Don't be tempted to make it stronger or you can actually damage your plants. You can buy the pipe from a builders' merchants.

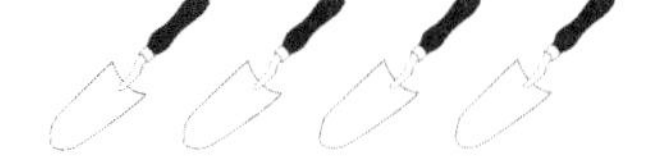

You will need

1 soil pipe end sleeve
1 soil pipe end cap
1 length of plastic soil pipe, about 11cm in diameter and 1.5m long
Glue suitable for plastic
Drill with 10mm drill bit
2 wall brackets with screws
Comfrey 'Bocking 14' plants
1 bamboo cane or stick
A waterproof container, such as a tin, about the same diameter as the pipe
2-pint plastic milk bottle with a side handle
Strong string or cord
A tile, brick or similar to keep rainwater out of the top of the pipe

When to do it

All year round

How to do it

Glue the end sleeve and cap onto one end of the pipe. Drill a hole in the centre of the cap – this is where the liquid will drip out, so a 10mm drill bit is the ideal size. Using the wall brackets, mount the pipe vertically against a wall, fence or shed, cap end down. Leave enough space at the bottom to fit in your container.

Gather your comfrey leaves and put them into the top of the pipe, pushing them down with a stick or cane so they reach the bottom.

Then place your container under the pipe. Fill the plastic bottle with water and tie one end of the string through the handle and the other end somewhere secure so it can't fall into the pipe. Make sure the string is as long as the pipe and lower the bottle into the pipe. This acts as a weight, keeping the leaves squashed down. Then place a tile or brick on the top of the pipe to stop rainwater getting in and diluting the feed.

After about three weeks, the leaves will break down and release a small amount of dark liquid which will drip into the container. Dilute this potassium-rich feed 40:1 and use it on your plants – particularly tomatoes and other fruiting crops. You can keep adding leaves into the top of the pipe whenever you like. Around once a year you can take the pipe down, empty out the mushy comfrey leaves and add them to your compost bin.

Pest control

Every garden has its share of unwelcome guests. Slugs, snails, leaf-munching caterpillars, aphids and moulds can lay waste to seedlings and weaken even mature plants. When you've said goodbye to your runner bean seedlings thanks to another night of slugs and snails, it can be tempting to rush to the garden centre and buy lots of powerful-looking chemicals to combat them. This is not only unnecessarily expensive but is also often ineffective and can even be harmful.

The healthiest gardens are those that have a good diversity of plant and animal life. A balanced ecosystem will have pests, sure, but also predators that can eat them. If you blast your aphids with a strong chemical you'll not only kill them but also the other beneficial insects such as ladybirds, hoverflies and lacewings that feed on them. And if you kill every single aphid in your garden, what are their predators supposed to eat? Encourage natural predators to thrive in your garden and trust that a balance will establish. You may have the odd chewed leaf and see a few blackfly and greenfly now and then, but in general your garden will be healthier and more robust if you practise natural control rather than opt for all-out annihilation. If you do find a particularly heavy infestation, try making safe, effective, pest-control solutions at home using stuff you probably already have in your kitchen cupboards.

Every pest has a natural predator. Work with nature rather than against it and you'll help your garden establish its own healthy balance.

10 tips for a naturally healthy garden

1. Plant plenty of pollinator-friendly flowers to encourage hoverflies, the larvae of which will eat aphids, mites, scale insects and caterpillars. Favourite hoverfly plants include fennel, ivy, Verbena bonariensis and any plant with daisy-like flowers.

2. Encourage birds into your garden as they will eat insect pests and slugs. Hang up bird feeders and plant berry-bearing trees and bushes such as rowan, crab apples, cotoneaster and honeysuckle, roses for hips and those with seed heads such as globe thistle, honesty and sunflowers.

3. Deter snails and slugs by removing their habitats: piles of pots are a favourite hiding place. Check under your garden pots and down the sides of raised beds for slugs and snails hiding there.

4. Keep a regular eye on your garden plants. If you spot a problem early it's much easier to treat it before it gets out of hand. If you see aphids, for example, squish them by hand or blast them off with a hose

5. Avoid fungal diseases such as mildew in crops by allowing space between them and keeping them well watered.

6. If you have space, allow an area of grass to grow long so that a rich diversity of wildlife can develop, or leave the edges of your garden to grow. You can mow it once a year if it gets too untidy. Don't banish nettles entirely either – they may make you a useful plant feed.

7. Keep your plants strong and healthy so they are less vulnerable to disease and pest attack by feeding the soil with garden compost, and your plants with home-made plant feeds.

8. Leave piles of logs, leaves and stones for ground beetles. They not only eat wireworms, chafer grubs, caterpillars and leatherjackets but adult slugs too.

9. Ladybirds also munch through a good few aphids – as adults and as larvae. Plant nectar- and pollen-rich flowers to encourage them. Herbs such as mint, dill, fennel and sage are ladybird favourites.

10. A healthy plant is more able to shrug off pest and disease attack; mulch plants in spring with garden compost or well-rotted manure to keep their nutrient levels up.

And if that doesn't work...

Problem pests and diseases and how to deal with them cheaply and organically

Slugs and snails

The bane of every gardener's life, slugs and snails are a particular problem for vegetable growers since a row of carrot seedlings can simply disappear overnight, causing much heartache and wailing. There are countless ways to deter them, ranging from the practical to the fanciful, but it really comes down to either attracting slugs and snails with something they find delicious (and then removing or killing them when you have them trapped) or killing them outright with shop-bought chemicals. The latter method is arguably easier and more effective; if you have particularly precious emerging seedlings, it might well be worth using slug pellets just until they have grown large enough to be more resilient to gastropod attack. Make sure the pellets are made from ferric phosphate, which is not harmful to other wildlife. Used sparingly, one bottle of these pellets will last you an entire growing season, maybe even two.

The best way to deal with snails is to look for them in their hiding places in the daytime. Check around the edges of raised beds and under or around pots and containers. Also check evergreen shrubs such as box. Then remove them by hand. What to do with them next? A firm heel will finish them off but will leave a bit of a mess. Throwing them over the garden fence is not very neighbourly (and might be ineffective since they can travel surprisingly long distances). I used to put them in a bowl of red wine but the resulting snail soup was so foetid and disgusting I couldn't bear to touch it, let alone know what to do with it. So now I tend to chuck them in my kitchen bin to be taken away with the other rubbish.

Slugs are less easy to spot, particularly since it's the little black inconspicuous ones that live underground that do most damage to young plants (they tend to have an orange underbelly). Those large slimy slugs you see on the pavement sometimes are actually fairly harmless, mainly eating dead plants not living ones. If you don't want to fork out for slug pellets – and only those based on ferric phosphate should be used if you don't want to harm other wildlife – these are your options, with pros and cons:

1. Oats. Good old porridge oats sprinkled around your plants are very tasty to slugs. When they eat them, however, the oats swell up inside them, killing them.
Pros: Cheap, easy to source.
Cons: Must be replaced regularly, you'll need a lot of oats to make a difference, it can get messy and rain may swell the oats before they get into the slugs.

2. Beer traps. Slugs and snails are attracted to the smell of beer (some people use wine or fruit juice instead) and will flock to it if you fill a pot and sink it into the ground. Leave a lip of a centimetre so ground beetles don't fall in and drown.
Pros: Cheap, easy to source.
Cons: Must be replaced regularly, disposal can be messy and smelly.

3. Start seedlings off in modules or small pots and only transplant them when they are big enough to be able to cope with the odd slug or snail nibble.
Pros: Effective.
Cons: Sowing direct is less time-consuming.

4. Plastic drink bottles make good protective collars to place around plants. Cut off the base and the narrow end with scissors and no slug would be able to scale that.
Pros: Free, effective.
Cons: Takes some time to prepare, finished collars not very pretty, can only cover selected plants and can blow over in wind.

5. Place melon rinds or grapefruit skins upside down in the bed. Slugs will gather there and can then be removed in the morning.
Pros: Free, as long as you don't buy the melons and grapefruit specially.
Cons: Must be replaced regularly, bit messy.

If you keep a bottle of wildlife-friendly slug pellets to hand for particularly precious seedlings, hunt and dispose of snails regularly and start some crops off in pots, only transplanting into beds when they are more resilient, you should avoid heartache.

above Oats are tempting to slugs and snails but will swell up inside them, killing them.

above Beer traps mean a sticky end for slugs and snails.

Aphids

Garden-centre shelves are packed with chemicals promising to blast aphids from your precious garden. In truth, aphids are much less damaging than many people think, since they tend to weaken rather than kill plants. It's true that by sucking sap from plants they make them more vulnerable to viruses and that leaves and shoots can look distorted and puckered as a result. It's also true that growth can be weakened. But aphids – those green, black or brown flies you see clustering around the tips of your roses, honeysuckle shoots and broad bean plants – are easily and very effectively dealt with by a blast of the garden hose. Repeat this every day and the attack should be beaten. Alternatively, if you're feeling brave, just squish the aphids between your fingers.

If you do want to go down the chemical route, you can buy insecticidal soft soap solution which is very effective and, if bought in a large bottle, good value. Buy it neat and dilute before applying. This organic soap won't harm other wildlife but will deal with aphids.

left Blast aphids off shoots with the garden hose every day until they are under control and you won't need to use chemicals.

Powdery mildew

If the leaves of your courgettes look like someone has sprinkled them with talcum powder, chances are it's powdery mildew, a fungal disease that members of the squash and cucumber family are particularly prone to. The mould prevents leaves from photosynthesising and it can quickly reduce even mature plants to limping specimens. It's made worse by poor ventilation (either cramped greenhouse conditions or plants positioned too close together) and dry roots, so keeping plants spaced appropriately and well watered can prevent it. But if you have mildew, you can eschew the various chemicals in the shops because help is at hand...

Make a spray for powdery mildew from milk

Scientists believe that the proteins in milk interact with the sun to create a brief antiseptic effect, burning any fungi that are present. To be effective the solution must be reapplied every ten days, in bright sunlight. It may be most effective if used preventatively before the fungus has taken a strong hold on the plant.

You will need
Milk
Water
A plastic spray bottle

When to do it
On a bright, sunny day

How to do it
Fill your bottle with equal parts milk and water and spray all affected areas, including the undersides of the leaves.

above Spray milk solution on affected leaves to tackle powdery mildew.

Leaf miner

If your chard and beetroot leaves suddenly develop wiggly tracks all over them, it's probably one of the many leaf miners that can cause a problem in gardens. The fly lays eggs on the underside of leaves (if you spot any, squash them) that then hatch into larvae that eat the inside of the leaf, making tunnels through them. An infestation can devastate a leafy crop like spinach or chard. No chemical purchases are necessary to combat this problem, though, just pull off the infected leaves and squash the larvae inside before adding them to the compost heap.

Carrot fly

The larvae of this fly can tunnel into carrots making them inedible. Signs of this pest are yellowing leaves and poor plant growth. Since the carrot fly is unable to fly more than about 36cm high, planting the crop in a tall container can prevent an infestation. Otherwise, cover the plants with a fine mesh or horticultural fleece. The flies are attracted to the smell of carrots, but you can disguise it by planting strong-smelling crops such as chives, garlic or onions near them. Bear in mind that for this to work you need as many of your companion plants as you do the carrots – which may mean rather a glut of chives! Alternatively, sow carrot-fly-resistant varieties such as 'Resistafly', 'Ibiza' or 'Sytan'.

Blight

This fungal disease can wipe out tomato and potato crops and is worse in wet, humid summers when conditions encourage the spores to spread. It is identified by brown patches on the leaves of the plants that gradually increase in size until the entire leaf and stem turns brown and rots. Potatoes underground will be ruined and tomatoes turn brown and decay. The bad news is that there is no cure for blight if you're unlucky enough to get it. Plants should be dug up, removed and burnt or thrown away (composting them will only return the spores to the soil). If you spot it early enough on potatoes (when only up to 25 per cent of the plant has been affected), you might be able to save the crop by cutting the plant right to the ground. Two weeks later, dig up the potatoes as usual. Planting blight-resistant potatoes such as 'Sarpo', will reduce your chances of an infestation. Alternatively, stick to First or Second Early potatoes, which mature before blight tends to make an appearance. In tomatoes, the early removal of affected leaves might stop it spreading.

Flea beetle

Brassicas such as cabbages and rocket can be affected by this little fly that peppers the leaves with tiny holes. If you touch the leaves, you'll see lots of little beetles jumping off. It won't kill mature plants but can make the leaves unappealing to eat, whereas seedlings can be wiped out. To catch them, smear some Vaseline onto a card and brush it over the plants. The beetles will hop off and get stuck on the card.

Scale insect

These shield-shaped bugs nestle under leaves or in the joints where stems meet the leaves where they look like little brown shells or scales. They suck the sap and weaken many plants and trees. They can be brushed off with an old toothbrush and soapy water.

Black spot

This fungus causes black spots on the leaves of roses, which gradually spread until the leaf yellows and falls off. The whole plant will then weaken. You can buy many sprays to avoid it, but if you don't want to fork out and/or use man-made chemicals that could harm other wildlife, you can keep this disease at bay with basic common sense. Avoid wetting the leaves when watering and remove any affected leaves as soon as you spot them. Throw these away rather than compost them. In autumn, when the leaves fall, rake them up and dispose of them – not on the compost heap. In spring, mulch around the base of the plants with a 10cm layer of well-rotted compost. This will bury any spores that may still be in the ground.

Rust

Rusts are fungal diseases that can be a particular problem for hollyhocks and snapdragons. Pear trees are also often affected. Signs are yellow, orange or brown pustules on leaves, usually on their undersides. Sometimes rusts cause little damage to the overall health of the plant, sometimes they can damage it severely, weakening growth. If only a few leaves are affected, removal of these will slow the spread of the disease. Avoid overcrowding plants, dispose of any affected material and try to keep foliage dry.

Damping off

It's a disappointing rite of passage for all budding gardeners. You sow some seeds in a module tray inside, smile as they germinate and then look on in anguish as they wither and die. What has happened? Chances are they've been hit by a fungal disease that has made them rot – known as 'damping off'. There's no cure, so prevention is the only solution.

To cut down on the chances of this happening, use only new commercial compost for seed sowing and clean pots between use. Use tap water not rainwater on seedlings to cut down the chances of fungal disease and try not to let the compost become waterlogged – it should be moist but not sopping. Watering from below – i.e. by placing pots in a container of water – rather than from above keeps the compost surface from getting too soggy.

Some people swear by using cold camomile tea as a preventative spray every other day. Others sprinkle cinnamon powder onto the soil surface. I can't vouch for either of these methods, but there would surely be no harm in trying? If your seedlings do die, throw away the compost and clean the pot or tray thoroughly with hot soapy water.

Resources

rhs.org.uk
The Royal Horticultural Society's online resource is full of useful gardening information from pruning and planting to how to train a fruit tree.

gardenorganic.org.uk
Charity championing organic gardening. Worth paying the modest membership fee to gain access to fact sheets on composting, soil management and other organic gardening techniques.

theseedsite.co.uk
Persevere through the rather serpentine web pages and you will find a wonderful image index of garden plants and weeds at their earliest seedling stages. Useful when weeding.

iacf.co.uk
International Antiques and Collectors Fairs will tell you when and where your nearest fair is. Ideal events for picking up vintage bargains for the garden.

carbootjunction.com
Car boot sales are great places to pick up deals - search here for a sale near you.

ebay.co.uk
gumtree.com
freecycle.org
Need no introduction – get your bargain/free plants, pots or gardening kit here.

seedysunday.org.uk
Home of Brighton's original seed swap event with advice for how to set up your own swap.

potato-days.net
It isn't just potatoes - there are plenty of seeds and plants to be swapped or bought at these UK-wide events.

realseeds.co.uk
This company not only sells very affordable vegetable seeds, but also gives good advice on seed saving.

musgrovewillows.co.uk
One of several, good value, willow suppliers.

pavingexpert.com
Plethora of free how-to advice on paving, paths and anything to do with hard landscaping in the garden.

organicplants.co.uk
Great value plug plants for an 'instant' veg patch.

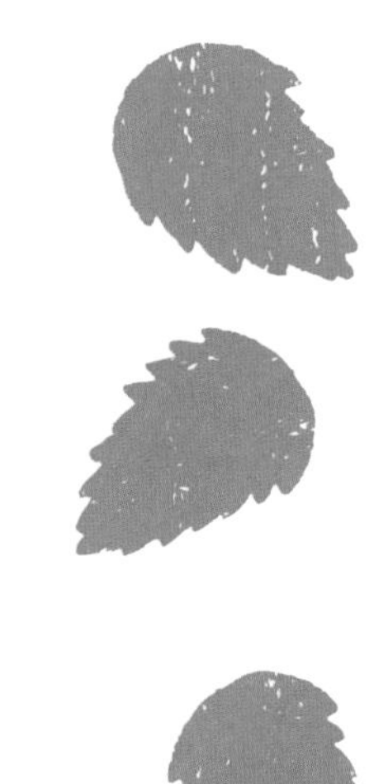

Index

Acknowledgements

To those behind the book: thank you Sarah, Judith, Kyle and Heather.

Many thanks to Amy, Will, Wendy, Paul and Jo for letting us take photos of your lovely gardens. And for the tea.

Not forgetting Dad for his splendiferous pelargonium, Karen for the tyre chat, Stuart for paving tips and Annette, Rachel and Sandra for saving their cans so I didn't have to get through a lifetime of tinned tomatoes in a month. Gratitude also due to the good shopkeepers of Borough Green – Wells Greengrocers for letting me nick their packing boxes and the guys at Kent Aluminium DIY who spent far more time than they needed to helping me devise a salad wall from a fruit crate.
True shoestringers all.